W9-DEJ-761

NEW DIRECTIONS FOR TEACHING AND LEARNING

Robert J. Menges, *Northwestern University*
EDITOR-IN-CHIEF

Marilla D. Svinicki, *University of Texas, Austin*
ASSOCIATE EDITOR

Classroom Assessment and Research: An Update on Uses, Approaches, and Research Findings

Thomas Angelo
DePaul University

EDITOR

Number 75, Fall 1998

JOSSEY-BASS PUBLISHERS
San Francisco

CLASSROOM ASSESSMENT AND RESEARCH: AN UPDATE ON USES, APPROACHES, AND RESEARCH FINDINGS
Thomas Angelo (ed.)
New Directions for Teaching and Learning, no. 75
Robert J. Menges, Editor-in-Chief
Marilla D. Svinicki, Associate Editor

ISSN 0271-0633   ISBN 0-7879-9885-0

NEW DIRECTIONS FOR TEACHING AND LEARNING is part of The Jossey-Bass Higher and Adult Education Series and is published quarterly by Jossey-Bass Inc., Publishers, 350 Sansome Street, San Francisco, California 94104-1342. Periodicals postage paid at San Francisco, California, and at additional mailing offices. Postmaster: Send address changes to New Directions for Teaching and Learning, Jossey-Bass Inc., Publishers, 350 Sansome Street, San Francisco, California 94104-1342.

New Directions for Teaching and Learning is indexed in College Student Personnel Abstracts, Contents Pages in Education, and Current Index to Journals in Education (ERIC).

SUBSCRIPTIONS cost $56.00 for individuals and $99.00 for institutions, agencies, and libraries. Prices subject to change.

EDITORIAL CORRESPONDENCE should be sent to the associate editor, Marilla D. Svinicki, The Center for Teaching Effectiveness, The University of Texas at Austin, Main Building 2200, Austin, TX 78712-1111.

Cover photograph by Richard Blair/Color & Light © 1990.

www.josseybass.com

CONTENTS

Since 1980, *New Directions for Teaching and Learning* has brought a unique blend of theory, research, and practice to leaders in postsecondary education. We strive not only for solid substance but also for timeliness, compactness, and accessibility.

Our series has the following goals:

1. To inform about current and future directions in teaching and learning in postsecondary education.
2. To illuminate the context that shapes those new directions.
3. To illustrate new directions through examples from real settings.
4. To propose how new directions can be incorporated into still other settings.

This publication reflects our view that teaching deserves respect as a high form of scholarship. We believe that significant scholarship is done not only by the researcher who reports results of empirical investigations but also by the practitioner who shares with others disciplined reflections about teaching. Contributors to NDTL approach questions of teaching and learning as seriously as they approach substantive questions in their own disciplines, dealing not only with pedagogical issues but also with the intellectual and social context out of which those issues arise. Authors deal with theory and research and with practice, and they translate from research and theory to practice and back again.

About This Volume. The authors in the present issue are advancing the work done in the area of classroom assessment and research since its initial introduction in the 1980s. Moving beyond the surface level of understanding of this movement, this issue looks at some foundational ideas that tie this work to the scholarship of teaching and the enhancement of learning. The methods themselves come under scrutiny in research aimed at their effects, and they are investigated in a wider range of situations than ever before.

ROBERT J. MENGES, *editor-in-chief, is professor of education and social policy, Northwestern University, and senior researcher, National Center on Postsecondary Teaching, Learning, and Assessment.*

MARILLA D. SVINICKI, *associate editor, is director, Center for Teaching Effectiveness, at the University of Texas at Austin.*

EDITOR'S NOTES

Classroom Assessment and Research began in the late 1980s as institutions were seeking ways of enlivening undergraduate teaching by reaching out to the teachers themselves. Who else could have such a direct impact on student learning? The first New Directions issue that focused on the process was *Classroom Research: Early Lessons from Success* (Angelo, 1991), which offered both an overview of the classroom research process and examples of its application in a wide range of settings. Since that time, faculty at hundreds of institutions have attempted some form of classroom research in their classes and realized the benefits of a more intense focus on student learning. Beyond that, classroom research itself has grown and matured as well.

The current issue examines some areas beyond the original conceptualization and use of classroom research. Like the teaching improvement it helps foster, classroom research has benefited from research and implementation in a wide array of settings and the data that result.

This issue begins with two conceptual explorations of Classroom Assessment and Research. In Chapter One, Cross discusses some foundational issues behind Classroom Assessment and Research and how it is realized in the classroom. But in addition, she shows how Classroom Assessment and Research can lead to and support the scholarship of teaching.

In the next chapter, Steadman and Svinicki turn the light of Classroom Assessment and Research from the teacher to the learner. They contend that the strategies can be woven into the fabric of a class so that students learn to use the techniques on their own to improve their learning if faculty point the way.

The next three chapters report results of research on Classroom Assessment and Research itself. In both the Steadman and the Soetaert chapters, attitudes of faculty and students toward Classroom Assessment and Research are described. Steadman's thorough studies look at Classroom Assessment and Research from both the teacher and the student perspective, while Soetaert relates the Classroom Assessment and Research process to the quality movement in higher education. The Cottell and Harwood chapter reports some interesting research results that could significantly affect how Classroom Assessment is implemented as an instructional aid.

The final section of the issue consists of an array of new uses and perspectives. Chapter Six, by Eisenbach, Golich, and Curry, compares how these three instructors from very different disciplines used similar assessment techniques to get both similar and dissimilar results, holding forth the possibility of a way to study *how* Classroom Assessment and Research functions. For Peterson and Stack, the new perspective was that of introducing Classroom Assessment and Research to an entire state system rather than a single classroom. Richlin describes the use of Classroom Assessment Techniques as a way to help beginning teachers develop their philosophies of teaching. Tebo-Messina and Van Aller show how Classroom Assessment and Research has helped an institution overcome resistance to calls for program accountability from the outside. The final chapter changes the focus of Classroom Assessment and Research from the class to the team, to show how many of the concepts can be used to promote good team work in students.

This issue illustrates that the philosophy of Classroom Assessment and Research has broad impact and implications. Classroom Assessment Techniques have moved well beyond tactics for use on a single class with a single problem. They represent instead a change in the way of thinking about teaching and learning and the relationship between them. I have no doubt that we have seen only a glimpse of what is possible when creative minds meet powerful strategies.

Reference

Angelo, T. A. *Classroom Research: Early Lessons from Success.* New Directions for Teaching and Learning, no. 46. San Francisco: Jossey-Bass, 1991.

THOMAS ANGELO *is associate professor and director of the Assessment Center at the School for New Learning, DePaul University.*

PART ONE

The Philosophy of Classroom
Assessment and Research

Classroom Assessment and Classroom Research play different roles in articulating the scholarship of teaching, but both hold great promise for impoving the conditions of learning in the classroom.

Classroom Research: Implementing the Scholarship of Teaching

K. Patricia Cross

In just a few years, the calendar will turn the page and open on not only a new year, but a new decade, a new century, and a new millennium! While much is being made of "the biggest deal in a thousand years," the year 2000 is only a number. But it is a number that seems to bring forth an unusually abundant rash of predictions about what the new century will bring *to* education—or more important, what the new century will require *from* education. What will higher education in the new century look like? Who will be in charge? What will be the agenda?

I am optimistic. I believe that the power to drive education will shift back onto the campus and away from outside sources like legislatures and accrediting agencies. People will conclude that good, strong education is run from inside—not from outside the institution. I believe that the twenty-first century will open with a broad theme of accepting responsibility for the quality of student learning. I believe that Classroom Assessment and Classroom Research can give faculty the tools to take on that responsibility and use it to their own advantage as well as that of their students and institutions.

One of the changes that is making this possible is a clear shift from assessment for accountability to assessment for improvement. In the early years of assessment, the compelling question for assessment planners was, What do *they* want? What sort of data must we collect to satisfy the requirements of accreditation review or state mandates? The new question emerging on many campuses is, What do *we* want to know about student learning so as to

---

Note: Excerpted from a presentation made at Washington State University, Pullman, Washington, September 12, 1996.

improve the quality of undergraduate education on this campus? Collecting assessment data on student learning outcomes for reporting to external others is one thing; collecting it for internal use in making changes is quite another. What happens on campus if the priority of the assessment movement shifts from doing assessment to using it to improve student learning?

Let's start with the obvious, but often ignored, fact that the folks who can actually do something to improve learning are teachers and students. Although assessment has many audiences, including legislators, accreditors, and the general public, in the final analysis, it is teachers and students, working together, who are ultimately responsible for the quality of learning.

Most institutions have worked conscientiously to get faculty involved in assessment, but students are rarely involved after they provide the data for analysis. Students are usually the subjects of assessment; rarely do we report back to them or involve them in the implementation. We must begin to include students as equal partners, sharing responsibility for the quality of learning.

Students should be included in the entire assessment process for two reasons. First, we can't improve student learning without the active and intelligent participation of students themselves. But second, and equally important, students as lifelong learners are going to have to assume more responsibility for their own learning. For most of a student's learning life, we—the formal educational establishment—are not going to be directing where, when, or what to learn. Today's students must, of necessity, become self-directed lifelong learners.

To date, teachers have assumed almost total responsibility for assessing student learning. But most teacher assessments tell students—often too little and too late—how they have done on a test or in a course, but not how they are doing as learners.

My colleague Tom Angelo and I have been working with college teachers from all kinds of colleges and from across the disciplines to develop some Classroom Assessment Techniques (CATs) that involve teachers and students in the direct assessment of classroom learning (Angelo and Cross, 1993). Classroom Assessment informs teachers how effectively they are teaching and students how effectively they are learning. Through Classroom Assessment, teachers get continual feedback on whether and how well students are learning what teachers hope they are teaching. And students are required, through a variety of Classroom Assessment exercises, to monitor their learning, to reflect on it, and to take corrective action while there is still time left in the semester.

Let me give an example of Classroom Assessment's most famous CAT. It is called the *minute paper,* and it works like this: Shortly before the end of a class period, the instructor asks students to write brief answers to these two questions: What is the most important thing that you learned in class today? and What is the main unanswered question you leave class with today?

Like most CATs, the minute paper is a teaching tool as well as an assessment device. It requires students to stop and think about what they have learned, to synthesize and articulate an important piece of learning, to express themselves in writing, and to think actively about what they did not understand. In short, it engages students in evaluating their own learning. If students are told that the minute paper is going to be requested at the end of a given class session, they may ask themselves along the way what they are learning and become more involved and more active in sorting out the major message. So even if the instructor failed to learn something important about teaching that class session, the minute paper would still be worthwhile for students, requiring them to reflect on their learning experience.

But teachers do learn a great deal from the feedback of the minute paper. Richard J. Light, director of the Harvard Assessment Seminars, reported that "this extraordinary idea is catching on throughout Harvard. Some experienced professors comment that it is the best example of high payoff for a tiny investment that they have ever seen" (Light, 1990, p. 36). The minute paper is now used in more than four hundred classes at Harvard. Indeed, the distinguished professor of statistics at Harvard, Frederick Mosteller, made his own contribution to the legends of CATs by inventing a version of the minute paper that he calls the *muddiest point*—an invitation to send a message to the instructor that many struggling students of statistics would find hard to resist (Mosteller, 1989).

The minute paper is used probably because it simple and easy to administer, but more fundamentally because it provides immediate feedback to both teachers and students about the learning that is taking place—or not taking place. Feedback is probably the single most important ingredient in improvement, whether used by teachers to improve their teaching or students to improve their learning. Consider, for example, the role of feedback in learning a skill such as archery.

Imagine a group of people who are trying to learn archery in a darkened room where both the target and feedback on hitting it are invisible. The archers may be provided with the best and most sophisticated equipment that money can buy; they may have one-on-one coaching from an expert teacher, and they may have access to good library materials on the history and practice of archery. Despite all this quality education on the input side, it's pretty clear that they are not going to improve their performance until they get some feedback on whether they are hitting the target.

We don't pay a lot of attention right now to giving students feedback on their progress as learners. Mostly, students get grades that tell them how they have done relative to their classmates. That information is not useful feedback on their progress as learners, nor does it do anything to help students develop skills for self-assessment. Classroom Assessment is a useful tool because it defines the target and provides useful feedback to students on their progress in hitting it.

If the improvement of learning is the priority for the twenty-first century, teachers and students need to be able to use the results of the assessment to improve their own performance. Now, what is it that they need to know?

Returning to the archery analogy, we need to turn the lights of assessment on both the target and the students' success in hitting it. Classroom Assessment can be targeted to provide feedback on whether students are accomplishing the goals that the teacher has in mind, but Classroom Assessment can also provide feedback on where student arrows are going astray. Are student arrows hitting the barn to the left of the target or the ground in front, or are they scattered all over the place? If feedback from the minute paper tells a teacher that students have no idea what the major message of the class session was or if student perceptions are distressingly different from teaching intentions, then a teacher wants to know why. For that we need Classroom Research.

At first, we used the terms Classroom Assessment and Classroom Research almost interchangeably, but we are now beginning to stress important distinctions between them. Classroom Assessment usually addresses the status quo or "what" questions of teaching and learning. *What* is going on in this class today? *What* did students learn from the day's lesson? *What* did they fail to understand or *what* did they have further questions about?

Classroom Research, in contrast, usually addresses understanding—the "why" and "how" questions about learning. *Why* did students respond as they did? *Why* did they hit the barn instead of the target? *Why* do they seem to have such foggy notions of where the target is? Broadly speaking, Classroom Research attempts to provide some insight into *how* students learn. It encourages teachers to use their classrooms as laboratories for the study of learning (Cross and Steadman, 1996).

Few college teachers know much about the learning process. For the most part, they have only their own experience as learners to guide them. And for most who choose academic life, learning has come easily. Such is not the case for many of today's students. The access revolution brought thousands of students into college classrooms who find academic learning difficult and threatening. If we in higher education are serious about taking responsibility for maximizing student learning, then teachers have to know more about how students learn. One way to do that is to carefully and systematically observe students in the process of learning what the teacher is trying to teach.

Faculty engaging in Classroom Research have much to contribute to our growing knowledge about human learning. There is an urgent need for research on teaching and learning in the disciplines. Teaching English at the college level is clearly different from teaching math. In fact, in our own research on teaching goals (Angelo and Cross, 1993), we found that faculty teaching priorities are related more to academic discipline than to any other factor. Teachers of a given discipline—whether male or female, full time or part time, experienced or inexperienced, teaching in a public community college or a private four-year college—share a value system with respect to teaching goals that is distinctively discipline-related and significantly different from that of colleagues in other disciplines.

While there are many characteristics that good college teachers share, and teachers can and should learn those generic teaching skills, it is quite clear that at the college level there is an enormous need for research on teaching in the disciplines. And no one is better qualified to do such research than college teachers who know their discipline and the problems in teaching it to undergraduates. By and large, the professions have recognized this, and there are now more than fifty discipline-specific pedagogical journals—*Physics Teacher, Teaching of Psychology, Research in the Teaching of English, Journal of Nursing Education,* and the like (Weimer, 1993).

Classroom Research differs in many ways from traditional research in or on classrooms. In the first place, it is not an add-on activity. It is embedded in the regular ongoing work of the class. Unlike research in the disciplines, which often requires special equipment and easy access to research libraries and colleagues engaged in cutting-edge research, college teachers doing research on learning have everything they need to do first-rate research. Most important, they have easy access to a population of students that is already engaged in just what the researcher wishes to study—learning a discipline under the realistic conditions of the classroom.

At its best, Classroom Research involves students as collaborators rather than subjects in the research. Knowledge about human learning, especially their own, is of high value and high interest to students. They are eager collaborators and the payoff for them is great in that they gain insight into their own learning while also developing the academic skills of inquiry and analysis.

Most important, Classroom Research differs from traditional educational research by completing the cycle from formulating the question to making changes in the practice of teaching. The typical pattern in traditional educational research has been for the investigator to do a research project, write up the findings, and publish them along with recommendations for someone else to carry out. This has been a notoriously ineffective design for the improvement of teaching and learning. Teachers are far too busy to read reports of research that seem to result in equivocal findings that may or may not apply to their students or their classrooms. One of the primary advantages of Classroom Research is that it is, by definition, relevant. It calls for the invention of a research question that the teacher finds interesting and important. And it is conducted in the relevant classroom, with the relevant students, in the relevant discipline. Let me give an example of a Classroom Research project cycle.

This example might start with an assessment using a CAT known as the *diagnostic learning log.* It asks students, usually as part of a homework assignment, to analyze their own learning process by answering a few questions such as these about the homework assignment (Cross and Steadman, 1996, p. 69):

1. Briefly describe the assignment you just completed. What do you think was the purpose of this assignment?
2. Give an example of one or two of your most successful responses. Explain what you did that made them successful.
3. Provide an example of where you made an error or where your responses were less complete. Why were these items incorrect or less successful?
4. What can you do differently when preparing next week's assignment?

The teacher might then prepare a tabulation of the responses, and together teacher and students would analyze the data. How well was the purpose of the assignment understood? Where did misunderstandings occur? What did students consider successful responses and why? Are there some common themes in the successful responses? Where were errors made? Are they common errors? To the extent that the assignment is typical or recurring, students will be interested in knowing how others are responding, and the project itself is both a learning experience and a descriptive study of the processes that are being used by students in the class.

Note that this design starts out fitting the definition of a traditional descriptive study; it tells how students responded to a brief questionnaire about a given assignment. But instead of stopping with the tabulation of the data—for example, 42 percent of the students misunderstood question 3— Classroom Research gives both teacher and students an opportunity to analyze the learning process. Interested and creative teachers will almost certainly find any number of questions and hypotheses for further investigation.

Consider, for example, the rich research possibilities involved in relatively simple data such as student responses to the question, "What do you think the purpose of the assignment is?" It is my guess that an insightful analysis of students' answers to that question would reveal considerable disparity. Some students would no doubt think the purpose of the assignment was to find the answer or to reproduce the information given in the assignment. Other students might think it was to understand a relationship or to critique an argument. Such observations tie into some interesting research being done in the British Commonwealth, primarily England and Australia, right now on deep versus surface learning (Ramsden, 1992; Gibbs, 1996). *Surface learning* refers to learners' attempts to reproduce information provided by others (often with the least possible effort), whereas *deep learning* refers to learners' attempts to understand and apply new information. In carrying out a relatively simple Classroom Research exercise, both teacher and students are engaging in the type of learning analysis that has long-term benefits. Research shows clearly that people who are aware of themselves as learners, that is, people who can watch themselves in the process of learning and analyze their responses, are better learners than those who are less aware of how they learn (Corno and Mandinach, 1983).

Another source of useful information that is free to classroom researchers—and rarely available to professional researchers—comes during office hours in the form of students with questions. Our usual response as teachers is to find out what they need explained and set about explaining it— often in the same way that did not work in the assignment or lecture. But that is the response of the teacher. The response of the researcher is different. The researcher is more likely to listen than to talk—to probe for insights about learning, to try to understand where the disconnect is between the presentation and the student's understanding. Sometimes, given half a chance to analyze their own learning, students will be remarkably insightful and articulate about a learning problem. More often, the researcher may need to launch some probing hypotheses, leading both researcher and student to a more analytical look at the learning process.

Fortunately in Classroom Research, an "N of one" may be more valuable than the N of hundreds needed to assure statistical significance in more traditional correlational research. An interview with a single student or a focus group with a small number of students or a discussion in a small class or seminar is more likely to result in an understanding of the process of learning than is a statistical study that may only tell us that certain things seem to be related. Worse yet, many traditional research studies are based on what Benjamin Bloom (1980) has called "unalterable variables"—variables such as age, ethnicity, and gender—that educators can do nothing to change. Granted, we may need to adapt to nontraditional unalterable characteristics, but they are not very helpful in understanding learning as a process. Classroom researchers are more interested in alterable variables, such as study strategies, teaching techniques, motivation, and other educational variables that can be changed by understanding and a willingness to learn about learning.

These brief and simple examples of Classroom Research should not be interpreted as constituting an amateur's research. Classroom Research, if it is to be effective, requires the careful launching and testing of insightful hypotheses. Its primary requirement is that it should benefit the participants, namely teachers and students, but it should also be related to broader themes about learning, themes that exist in the literature on learning and in the experiences and experiments of teaching colleagues. While Classroom Research may or may not be published, it should be of a quality and interest worthy of credibility and other people's attention. (See Cross and Steadman, 1996, for the relationship of Cognitive Research to Classroom Research.)

And that brings me to some concluding comments about the Classroom Research community. Research is often considered a solitary activity, taking academics out of the classroom to the lab or library to do their work in isolated splendor. While it is perfectly possible to do Classroom Research within the confines of one's own classroom, we are finding that once faculty start down the road of Classroom Research, they are eager to share the experience with their colleagues. After all, teaching is one thing that faculty have in common. It is a paradox that teaching in higher education is such a strangely private affair. It is learned in private and for the most part practiced in private without much input or conversation with others engaged in the same activity.

Classroom Research provides a stimulus to forming a community around the mission that all colleges and universities share, and that is teaching. At the first level, there is the collaboration and discussion with students about learning, which is, after all, the common purpose shared by teachers and students. At the next level, there is departmental and interdepartmental research about student learning, which is the common purpose of departments and divisions. At still another level, there is the community formed by the disciplines. I have already remarked that the disciplinary professions are newly engaged in the publication and sharing of information about teaching and pedagogy through specialized disciplinary journals and the Internet. Classroom Research can only be enhanced by sharing both the investigations and the outcomes with students and teaching colleagues.

In conclusion, I believe that college teaching is a scholarly profession that will come into its own in the twenty-first century. The members of a profession are bound together through sharing a base of knowledge and experience that makes them qualified to exercise judgment and skill in the practice of their profession. Strangely missing from the profession of teaching as we close out this century is the ability to advance the profession through a shared base of knowledge about human learning. Classroom Research has the potential for creating teaching and learning communities with the shared goal of understanding learning well enough to improve it—as individual classroom teachers and as collective faculties dedicated to the mission of improving undergraduate education.

References

Angelo, T. A., and Cross, K. P. *Classroom Assessment Techniques: A Handbook for College Teachers.* (2nd ed.) San Francisco: Jossey-Bass, 1993.

Bloom, B. "The New Direction in Educational Research: Alterable Variables." *Phi Delta Kappan,* Feb. 1980, pp. 382–385.

Corno, L., and Mandinach, E. "The Role of Cognitive Engagement in Classroom Learning and Motivation." *Educational Psychologist,* 1983, *18* (2), 88–108.

Cross, K. P., and Steadman, M. H. *Classroom Research: Implementing the Scholarship of Teaching.* San Francisco: Jossey-Bass, 1996.

Gibbs, G. *Improving Student Learning.* Oxford, England: Oxford Centre for Staff Development, Oxford Brookes University, 1996.

Light, R. J. *The Harvard Assessment Seminars.* Cambridge, Mass.: Harvard University, 1990.

Mosteller, F. "The 'Muddiest Point in the Lecture' as a Feedback Device." *On Teaching and Learning: The Journal of the Harvard-Danforth Center,* Apr. 1989, pp. 10–21.

Ramsden, P. *Learning to Teach in Higher Education.* New York: Routledge, 1992.

Weimer, M. "The Disciplinary Journals on Pedagogy." *Change,* 1993, *25,* 44–51.

K. PATRICIA CROSS is David Pierpont Gardner Professor of Higher Education, University of California, Berkeley.

Classroom Assessment opens the opportunity for more than just the improvement of teaching. With a solid grounding in learning theory, it has the potential of helping students become better learners as well.

CATs: A Student's Gateway to Better Learning

Mimi Steadman, Marilla Svinicki

At present, many faculty learn about Classroom Assessment Techniques (CATs) by observing other more experienced faculty members modeling a variety of CATs for colleagues. While modeling is extremely useful for demonstrating the "what" or "how" of Classroom Assessment, it is less successful at conveying the "why" of Classroom Assessment. Faculty members who wish to get the maximum benefit from Classroom Assessment are well-advised to learn about the relationship between CATs and cognitive learning theory. Understanding this link will not only allow them to choose or design CATs to fit the particular needs of their classes, it will also help them make explicit to their students the potential applications of CATs to study strategies in general. Once a student can make this leap, the effects of a single class activity are multiplied many times.

Cognitive Learning Theory

The theory that connects Classroom Assessment to learning is cognitive learning theory. Cognitive theory focuses on what is going on in the mind of the learner rather than thinking of learning as a simple stimulus-response connection. In this theory the learner is an active participant in the learning process; indeed, in some versions of cognitive theory, learning is almost completely a function of the learner's interpretation of events.

   In its most general form, the theory describes learning as a building of connections between a learner's prior knowledge and experience and the new information or skill that is being learned. A successful learning episode results in the assimilation of new information into the long-term memory structure of the learner via these connections. Later, when the new information is needed, the learner will activate any one of a number of these connections and the information will be retrieved for use.

There are several key processes in the building of connections during learning. These three are most important from the perspective of this chapter:

- *Attention:* For information to be learned, the learner must focus attention on it.
- *Encoding (deep processing):* The learner transforms the information in ways that will make it more meaningful, more connectable, and therefore more retrievable. The most common ways of encoding information involve recognizing or imposing organization on it; elaborating on it by adding information from the learner's background; creating a memorable visual image that represents the information; and (least efficient) rehearsing it until it has been rote memorized, a strictly surface processing technique.
- *Metacognition:* The learner is aware of and in active control of his or her own learning. This is manifest in goal setting (understanding or deciding why something needs to be learned and setting the standard by which progress will be measured); comprehension monitoring (recognizing when one isn't learning and why); strategy selection (being able to select from an array of learning strategies those most likely to achieve the goal); and resource management (being aware of and able to bring a wide range of resources into play in achieving the goal).

The Link to Classroom Assessment

Most of the Classroom Assessment Techniques recommended in Angelo and Cross (1993) are tied in some way to this model of learning. A very thorough discussion of the subject is found in Cross and Steadman's (1996) *Classroom Research: Implementing the Scholarship of Teaching,* which contains case studies addressing universal learning issues in a variety of higher education classrooms and reviews of the literature on learning theory.

When an instructor employs one of the CATs, he or she can use the experience at several levels. There is the feedback to the instructor on instruction that has been the primary focus of this issue, of course. But at the same time, the student is usually getting feedback on his or her own learning of the specific content.

One step up the metacognitive ladder from these two very concrete levels is the opportunity for the CAT to improve the students' monitoring of their own comprehension, a key metacognitive skill. Several authors in this issue note that when students are constantly being asked to provide feedback to the instructor on their learning, they develop the habit of checking that learning periodically on their own so as to be ready to respond to the request for feedback. This often becomes a conscious habit, and this is more likely to happen when the instructor can make it more conscious by directly discussing the possibility with the students regularly.

The next step up the ladder is when students take the comprehension monitoring strategies they have learned in one class and transfer them to other learning episodes, such as when studying alone or with friends, or when participating in another course. This would be facilitated if several instructors began using CATs as learning tools. Seeing them in multiple settings would help students make the transfer of these strategies more readily.

Table 2.1 shows how each of the most commonly used CATs might contribute to learning as conceived of in cognitive theory. In reality each CAT has several possible connections to the learning process. Almost all will focus student attention on key concepts to be learned. Most are also very helpful in articulating ways in which information to be learned can be organized and elaborated on for better storage. The very act of doing a CAT is often the opportunity for increasing metacognitive awareness in students. The repeated use of a particular CAT can establish patterns of thinking about the material that would usually not occur, especially if the instructor makes a point of clarifying the thinking behind its use.

Examples of Using CATs to Enhance Learning

One possible use of CATs would be in large introductory lectures. Faculty might use the *punctuated lecture* CAT (Angelo and Cross, 1993, p. 303). In this technique the teacher stops in midlecture and asks students to reflect on their

Table 2.1. Commonly Used CATs and Their Connection to Cognitive Theory

CAT	Connections to Cognitive Theory
Minute paper	Metacognition—comprehension monitoring Rehearsal of key ideas Organization of knowledge—identifying main points
Muddiest point	Metacognition—comprehension monitoring
Categorizing grid	Organization of knowledge—identifying critical attributes of concepts
Directed paraphrasing	Elaboration—putting things in learner's own words Meaningful connections
Diagnostic learning logs	Metacognition—awareness of strategies; evaluation of strategy use
Concept maps	Organization of knowledge—identifying connections and key ideas Elaboration—making connections
Memory matrix	Rehearsal of key words

learning and listening behavior during the presentation. Students take a few moments to write down their reflections, then share this feedback anonymously with the instructor. Punctuated lecture forces students to reflect on their classroom learning behaviors, and to self-assess their level of comprehension of new material.

The instructor might then prepare a mini-lesson to follow the punctuated lecture CAT by introducing students to the idea of metacognition. Exhibit 2.1 illustrates the ideas that an instructor might include in a discussion of metacognition as illustrated by the punctuated lecture.

In another example of using a CAT to change student study behavior, as a review for an exam, the instructor might project a list of key words that make

Exhibit 2.1. Mini-Lesson on Metacognitive Strategies to Follow Up the Punctuated Lecture CAT

Instructor describes the Learning Strategy: Metacognition is "thinking about thinking" and controlling your learning. This relates to how often you think about what you are hearing, reading, or studying. For example, did you have a hard time describing what you were doing during this lecture when I asked you to just now? Did you find that you were thinking about something else rather than listening and thinking about what I was saying? What did you do to focus your attention on the lecture if you did find yourself drifting? The same thing applies when you are studying at home. Do you monitor your attention while you read, or do you often find that you have read ten pages in your textbook and can't remember any of it? Do you adjust your reading speed if you're reading something difficult versus reading for pleasure?

Instructor offers suggestions for using the Strategy: In listening to lectures, pay particular attention at the beginning because most instructors start the lecture with an overview of what will be discussed. Write down what the purpose of the lecture is. This will help you keep yourself focused during the lecture itself. When you find yourself drifting, go back and reread the purpose and see if you can relate what is being said to that purpose. When you have reading to do, skim the material before you begin to see how it is organized. Look at the headings and subheadings of the text to give yourself an idea of how things are related to each other. While reading, ask yourself questions about the paragraph you have just read and scribble keywords in the margins of the book or in a notebook. This will work during lectures, too. Conduct "punctuated study sessions" just like the one we just did to monitor your study behaviors and understanding on your own. Try to determine which concepts you don't understand well. Although this method takes longer initially, you are more likely to remember what you have read or heard. This saves you time later when studying for a test.

Note: The learning strategy description and suggestions in this exhibit and the ones that follow are partially based on the student feedback section in *A Manual for the Use of the Motivated Strategies for Learning Questionnaire* by Pintrich, Smith, Garcia, and McKeachie (1991).

up the primary concepts of the unit and have the students create concept maps that link the ideas and illustrate the relationships between them (Angelo and Cross, 1993, p. 197). The focus in *concept mapping* is on the relationship among the concepts rather than on the concepts themselves. This forces students to move beyond mere memorization to more relational thinking. In fact, if the instructor begins using the concept mapping strategy as the organizational structure for presenting the material as well, students might have an easier time focusing on relationships in their learning. Again, the instructor can follow up this CAT with a discussion of studying for exams that goes beyond mere memorization or surface learning.

Instead of starting with a CAT and following up with a learning strategy lesson, faculty can start with the learning skills they wish to promote, and then choose CATs that can help students develop those skills. For example, the two worksheets in Exhibit 2.2 and Exhibit 2.3 require an instructor to generate a list of CATs and other learning activities that can encourage students' use of two valuable learning strategies: elaboration and organization.

Another resource in the *Classroom Assessment Handbook* (Angelo and Cross, 1993) is the *teaching goals inventory,* a self-scorable instrument that faculty can use to reflect on and prioritize their objectives for teaching. The teaching goals inventory (TGI) is organized into six clusters of goals for student learning that faculty may choose to emphasize in their teaching: higher-order thinking skills, basic academic success skills, discipline-specific knowledge and skills, liberal arts and academic values, work and career preparation, and personal development.

Faculty are encouraged to use CATs as tools to assess how successfully they are meeting their teaching goals. CATs can also be used as tools in faculty's efforts to achieve those goals. For example, teachers whose goals focus on imparting discipline-specific knowledge and skills could use CATs like the memory matrix (Angelo and Cross, 1993, p. 142) not only to assess whether students have retained course content but also to help students rehearse and retain new material. Faculty interested in assessing and enhancing students' development of higher-order thinking skills may use more complex CATs like approximate analogies (Angelo and Cross, 1993, p. 193) or invented dialogues (Angelo and Cross, 1993, p. 203).

Next Steps

Instructors who wish to learn more about learning theory can, in addition to reviewing the Angelo and Cross (1993) and Cross and Steadman (1996) books, look into just about any textbook on psychology, educational psychology, or cognitive psychology. Most of these sources are designed for those just beginning in the field, so they will be an easy read for faculty in any discipline. Getting together with other faculty and discussing the ideas behind CATs and the theory would also be a very useful way to come to an understanding of alternative ways of using these ideas.

Exhibit 2.2. Learning Theory Application: Elaboration Strategies

Explicit Learning Strategy Instruction for Students

Description of the Learning Strategy

Elaboration strategies are your attempts to summarize or paraphrase the material you read in your textbooks, and to relate the material to what you already know or have learned. These strategies usually result in better performance than rehearsal strategies alone because they help learners make meaningful connections with existing knowledge.

Suggestions for Using this Strategy

Paraphrase and summarize important information. Use your own words to describe the material covered during lecture or in assigned reading. Pretend you're the teacher and are trying to explain the topic to students. Try to figure out how each topic relates to others. What are the connections between what you've heard in lecture, talked about in discussion, read in the textbook, or learned from your own experiences?

Connecting Learning Theory and Classroom Practice

CAT Connections

Muddiest point
Minute paper
Punctuated lecture
Concept map
Word journal
Analytic memos
Applications cards
Approximate analogies
Directed paraphrasing, etc.
(Angelo and Cross, 1993)

What other strategies might students use in class and while studying to improve their learning skills in this area?

Small group discussions
Peer tutoring
Free writing (students spend five
  minutes in class writing about a
  course topic or question in their
  own words)
Pair and share (students explain a
  course concept to a partner)

Once an instructor has begun to delve beneath the surface of Classroom Assessment, there is much to reward the effort. Ultimately, the instructor will be able to design CATs that are targeted at a given course or concept and will no longer have to rely on or adapt the existing CATs. At that point the instructor's scholarship of teaching will allow a much greater appreciation that something *can* be done to improve student learning, not just in a given class but in general.

Exhibit 2.3. Learning Theory Application: Organization Strategies

Explicit Learning Strategy Instructions for Students

Description of the Learning Strategy

Organizational strategies help learners condense large amounts of new information and make sense of relationships among new concepts and existing knowledge. Organizational strategies include outlining information, such as a chapter in a book or concepts from a lecture. Another form of organization is creating diagrams, perhaps of a scientific process, a chain of events, or related course concepts. Clustering ideas into categories that indicate shared characteristics is another organizational strategy.

Suggestions for using this strategy

Outline course material and identify where the text and lecture overlap and don't overlap. This will give you a starting point in developing connections between ideas presented in two different contexts. Make charts, diagrams, or tables of important concepts. A flow chart or a tree diagram may help you understand how different ideas fit together.

Connecting Learning Theory and Classroom Practice

CAT Connections

Concept maps
Memory matrix
Defining features matrix
One-sentence summary
Problem recognition task
What's the principle? (Angelo and Cross, 1993)

Building bridges (Cross and Steadman, 1996)

What other strategies might students use in class and while studying to improve their learning skills in this area?

Card sorting
Venn diagrams
Color coding concepts

References

Angelo, T. A., and Cross, K. P. *Classroom Assessment Techniques: A Handbook for College Teachers.* (2nd ed.) San Francisco: Jossey-Bass, 1993.

Cross, K. P., and Steadman, M. H. *Classroom Research: Implementing the Scholarship of Teaching.* San Francisco: Jossey-Bass, 1996.

Pintrich, P. R., Smith, D.A.F., Garcia, T., and McKeachie, W. J. *A Manual for the Use of the Motivated Strategies for Learning Questionnaire.* (Tech. Report No. 91–B–004). Ann Arbor: Regents of the University of Michigan, School of Education, National Center for Research to Improve Postsecondary Teaching and Learning, 1991.

MIMI STEADMAN is a private consultant on Classroom Assessment and Classroom Research working out of the New York area after leaving the University of California at Berkeley.

MARILLA SVINICKI is director of the Center for Teaching Effectiveness at the University of Texas at Austin and a senior lecturer in educational psychology.

PART TWO

Research on Classroom
Assessment and Research

Research indicates that Classroom Assessment affects the experiences
of both the teacher and the students.

Using Classroom Assessment to Change Both Teaching and Learning

Mimi Steadman

Those who have used Classroom Assessment over the past several years are confident about one thing: Classroom Assessment is good for both teachers and students. As a feedback strategy that provides teachers with data on teaching effectiveness and student comprehension, Classroom Assessment also involves students in active mental processing of new information and makes them more aware of themselves as learners. Classroom Assessment (Angelo and Cross, 1993; Cross and Angelo, 1988) is an educational innovation that unites efforts to improve both teaching and learning.

A Study of Classroom Assessment Techniques in Community Colleges

For nearly ten years faculty have informally communicated the teaching and learning benefits of Classroom Assessment to their colleagues. *Classroom Assessment Techniques: A Handbook for College Teachers* (Angelo and Cross, 1993) contains several rich case studies that illustrate Classroom Assessment in practice, and Angelo (1991) compiled a number of reports on the successful implementation of Classroom Assessment in an earlier *New Directions for Teaching and Learning* volume. To complement the positive anecdotal reports on Classroom Assessment, a few formal studies have been conducted. For example, Catlin and Kalina (1993) addressed student retention and perception of classroom

Note: This research was supported through the practitioner-based research fellowship program of the National Center on Adult Learning, Empire State College, Saratoga Springs, New York.

environment, and found slight increases in retention and higher student reports of involvement, cohesiveness, satisfaction, and task understanding in courses where CATs were used. Cuevas (1991) followed up community college instructors who were enrolled in his course on Classroom Research, and found that the most frequent use of Classroom Assessment was for assessing teaching practice, while others used classroom assessment to develop and assess student learning skills. Diana Kelly conducted dissertation research on Classroom Assessment in which she trained community college faculty in Classroom Assessment and concluded that it "enhances faculty vitality and encourages greater interest and involvement in teaching" (1993, p. 198). Kelly also studied student involvement, but was unable to document statistically significant increases there. Nevertheless, open-ended student survey data revealed positive student feelings about learning progress and involvement.

In this chapter I summarize the results of a study (Steadman, 1994a, 1994b) on the implementation and impact of CATs in community colleges, where CATs have been especially popular and widely implemented. I was interested in building on earlier work by addressing both sides of the teaching and learning equation, looking at faculty *and* student experiences with Classroom Assessment. I sought out common threads in faculty and student self-reported experiences that could reveal why Classroom Assessment techniques were described in anecdotal reports as beneficial to student learning and satisfaction.

I investigated faculty and student experiences with Classroom Assessment in three ways. First, I explored how Classroom Assessment has been applied in practice by community college teachers, documented changes in teaching behaviors, and considered the costs and benefits of Classroom Assessment for teachers. Second, I explored the experiences and satisfaction of community college students in courses taught by teachers who incorporate Classroom Assessment activities. Finally, I investigated the potential of Classroom Assessment Techniques to promote student metacognition and the use of learning strategies.

Methodology

For this project, I combined surveys, interviews, and observations of community college faculty and students. The research was conducted during the fall 1993 semester at three community colleges in Northern California with student populations diverse in terms of age, ethnicity, and academic preparation. There were four major components of the methodology: a survey of 136 faculty members from thirty-five California community colleges, selected from a directory of teachers involved in Classroom Assessment (56 responded for a response rate of 41 percent); interviews with 9 community college teachers using Classroom Assessment at three college sites; a beginning and end-of-semester (pre-test/post-test) survey of 164 community college students enrolled in classes taught by the 9 instructors in the faculty interview sample; and interviews with 9 students from the student survey sample.

Student surveys included demographic items, questions about their satisfaction with the course, as well as items from selected scales on an instrument that measures students' use of learning strategies—the Motivated Strategies for Learning Questionnaire (MSLQ) (Pintrich, Smith, Garcia, and McKeachie, 1991). Student responses from pre-test to post-test surveys were tracked by social security number so we could measure changes on learning strategies scores, and so that students could be provided with feedback on their responses to the pre-test survey along with suggestions for improving their study skills. Finally, the project included observations of classrooms and of meetings of Classroom Assessment groups (groups of faculty meeting for training in or collaboration on Classroom Assessment) at two colleges.

Research Findings: Classroom Assessment and Faculty Experience

Faculty purpose affects Classroom Assessment practice. The faculty surveyed and interviewed in this research communicated thoughtful and goal-driven purposes for using Classroom Assessment in their efforts to improve teaching and learning. For example, when an ESL teacher wanted to encourage her most reticent students—some of whom were from cultures where the teacher is always right—to voice their opinions about the class, she administered a teacher-designed feedback form for them to complete anonymously. A composition teacher, confronted with a class with wide variations in preparation levels, administered a background knowledge probe to figure out how much review she would need to do at the beginning of the semester. A key finding of this study was that faculty purposes for using Classroom Assessment influenced how they implemented CATs, what subsequent changes they made in their teaching, and how they perceived the impact of this innovation.

The five most frequently mentioned purposes for using Classroom Assessment are summarized in the following list, along with illustrative quotes from open-ended survey and interview responses, to the question "Why do you use Classroom Assessment?"

An instructor's purpose for using Classroom Assessment was the engine that drove implementation choices. What faculty put into Classroom Assessment determined what they got out of it. And, the effort that faculty devoted to Classroom Assessment depended on their goals for using it. For example, some faculty devoted their implementation of CATs to gaining feedback on students' perceptions of instruction, using techniques that can be characterized as "customer survey" CATs. These teachers, who relied on CATs like the instructor-designed feedback form, reported that they gained valuable insights from students' reactions to instruction, and in many cases changed instructional approaches. One teacher compared CATs to trucks on the freeway with

Purpose for Using Classroom Assessment	Sample Interview or Survey Responses
To obtain feedback on the effectiveness of and student satisfaction with teaching and classroom activities	"Well, it does give me feedback that otherwise, when you're up there all by yourself just doing your own thing, you don't get. It allows you to see what you're doing through the eyes of the people who are sitting there in class."
To improve teaching	"Well, I think it really helps me, it makes me a better teacher, and I think it helps the students get more out of the class. So that's my main motivation."
To monitor students' learning	"To check that the students are actually learning or retaining the material presented. Also to see if they are getting what I *think* I'm giving them."
To improve students' learning (in terms of retention or learning skills)	"Well, I use it for the reason it was intended—to improve their learning."
To improve communication and collaboration with students	"It makes classrooms much more collaborative—students feel that they're part of the act."

bumper stickers that ask "How am I driving? Call 1-800-4-Safety." She says, "That's what I ask my students, 'How am I doing? Here's your CAT, let me know.'"

Other faculty used CATs like the minute paper or the one sentence summary (Angelo and Cross, 1993, p. 183) in an effort to monitor students' understanding of new course content, and to provide students an opportunity to reflect on and synthesize new learning. These faculty more often reported that the use of CATs increased student involvement and student learning. Ideally, given Angelo and Cross's intentions that CATs be learning as well as assessment activities, faculty will begin to tap into Classroom Assessment's potential to enhance student learning in addition to providing feedback on instruction.

Advantages of Classroom Assessment for Faculty. The most frequently mentioned advantage of Classroom Assessment was the ability to *tune in to students' voices* and as a result, having students who are more satisfied because they know their teachers care. One respondent commented: "Our students feel they have a voice in the classroom. They feel that their instructor does care about their learning." This first advantage of Classroom Assessment is closely related to the changes teachers reported making as a result of using the procedure, including assessing more and increasing collaboration and communication with students.

The second most frequently mentioned advantage was *the opportunity to engage in reflection on and systematic change of their teaching.* A faculty interviewee explained: "I feel that I have some power, in that I can really organize, orchestrate the class, and I know what techniques I can use. . . . So I'm not so much reacting anymore, I'm directing." This advantage is especially meaningful to those teachers who reported improving teaching as their purpose for using Classroom Assessment, and corresponds to reported changes in classroom activities, teaching style, and presentation and review of new material.

A third advantage was *student improvement and involvement in learning.* One survey respondent wrote that "students are more likely to learn the material—that keeps them involved in the class." I will return to a discussion of benefits to students later in this chapter.

The fourth major advantage of Classroom Assessment was *the opportunity to join a community of other faculty committed to teaching.* Although Classroom Assessment was originally designed so that it could be implemented in the privacy of one's own classroom, without direction or evaluation from others, these teachers' initial introduction to Classroom Assessment was through ongoing Classroom Assessment groups at their colleges. Interviewees credited Classroom Assessment for "making teaching a priority again" and described Classroom Assessment faculty groups as the only place in the college "where you ever discuss teaching."

Disadvantages of Classroom Assessment for Faculty. In survey and interview data, only two disadvantages, time and negative feedback, were consistently reported, and several respondents left the disadvantage item blank. In Catlin and Kalina's study (1993, p. 55), forty-five out of forty-six faculty reported that there were "absolutely no negative experiences" associated with their use of CATs. The main disadvantage of Classroom Assessment that emerged in this study was "so many CATs, so little time." Respondents noted the time required for planning, administering, and analyzing CATs. In addition to the time required to administer a CAT, if teachers discover that students did not understand a particular lesson, additional class time may be required to review and clarify concepts.

The second disadvantage that faculty reported was dealing with negative feedback. One form that negative feedback can take is criticism of teaching in response to faculty requests for student comments on their satisfaction with teaching and classroom activities. Survey respondents warned that "one must be willing to take criticism" and "you might find out you are not teaching as well as you want." Nevertheless, faculty concluded that the information gained from CATs was valuable, even when it was surprising or discouraging. As one teacher explained: "It's good, because you would never have known it if you hadn't done it."

These findings highlight three key lessons:

Classroom Assessment is an intrinsically rewarding activity for faculty. Research has shown teaching to be an intrinsically motivating activity for community college faculty (Frase and Piland, 1989). One reason for Classroom Assessment's widespread appeal is that it capitalizes on teachers' existing motivation to teach as well as they can. The faculty in this study report that opportunities for learning, reflection, and improvement are highly motivating as well.

In this study, I was interested in what motivates faculty to adopt and implement an innovation like Classroom Assessment. The findings confirmed that Classroom Assessment is an instructional innovation that possesses several characteristics noted by Rogers (1983) and Kozma (1979) in their research on the adoption of innovations as contributing to rapid adoption rates. Perhaps the most important characteristic of a teaching innovation like Classroom Assessment that contributes to its adoption, continued use, and faculty satisfaction is that according to faculty reports, it is an intrinsically rewarding activity.

Faculty appreciated the feedback they received from Classroom Assessment, as well as the opportunity to try a variety of techniques depending on their skills and interests. Another aspect of Classroom Assessment's broad appeal was a result of instructors' ability to implement CATs according to their individual goals, interests, and time available for planning and analysis. What faculty perceived as benefits of Classroom Assessment match three attributes of intrinsically rewarding activities: task demands matching individuals' skill levels, range of challenges, and feedback (Csikszentmihalyi, 1982). The list of benefits of Classroom Assessment (the ability to tune in to student voices, improved student learning, opportunities for reflection and change, and a faculty community) supports the premise that faculty undertake certain instructional innovations because of the intrinsic rewards they derive from teaching and interacting with students (Kozma, 1979).

When I asked faculty what would motivate them to use Classroom Assessment more extensively or more often, they were especially interested in incentives such as release time to carry out significant Classroom Assessment projects, the opportunity to substitute Classroom Assessment for other committee or administrative responsibilities, and support to attend workshops and conferences. These incentives can be construed as either intrinsic or extrinsic rewards. For example, release time and substitution would be considered intrinsic rewards if faculty derive satisfaction from the opportunity to carry out additional or more elaborate Classroom Assessment activities. On the other hand, if the major satisfaction derived from release time or substitution of responsibilities is avoiding other work rather than enjoying Classroom Assessment itself, these motivating factors could be viewed as extrinsic. Faculty did not rate stipends, which are clearly extrinsic incentives, as highly motivating. But given increasing workloads and shrinking budgets, my hunch is that they probably would not refuse stipends, either.

One surprising finding, in light of community college faculty members' emphases on teaching and belief that they should be evaluated on their teaching effectiveness (Carnegie Foundation for the Advancement of Teaching, 1989), was that 86 percent of faculty respondents indicated that they would be "somewhat" or a "great deal" motivated by the opportunity to publish results of their Classroom Assessment work. Most disciplines have a journal on pedagogy as a potential outlet for such articles.

Classroom Assessment promotes reflective practice in teachers. Classroom Assessment provided faculty the opportunity to reflect on their teaching and to make informed changes in instruction. Eighty-eight percent of faculty surveyed reported that they had made changes in their teaching behaviors as a result of Classroom Assessment. The four major categories of changes in teaching that emerged from faculty survey and interview data were assessing more or assessing at all, changing classroom activities or teaching style, modifying presentation and reviewing new material, and increasing communication and collaboration with students.

For some faculty, Classroom Assessment was the first time they had ever asked students for feedback, while other faculty said that they had always made an effort to assess learning, but used CATs to do so more frequently and more effectively. Changes in teaching style and classroom activities as a result of student feedback included speaking more slowly and writing on the board, as well as incorporating different activities such as group projects or student-generated test questions into their classes. Modifying presentation and review of new material was a change that resulted when teachers used CATs to monitor student learning and discovered that students were not learning what faculty thought they were teaching. Faculty also reported developing new formats for the organization, presentation, and review of course content. The final reported change in teaching was that teachers felt that they had opened lines of communication with students, and involved students more in the organization of the class.

Classroom Assessment, therefore, seems to have contributed to faculty's development as reflective practitioners (Schön, 1983) who engage in ongoing inquiry and discovery about their work as teachers. Echoing Schön's view that a reflective practitioner "engages in a continuing process of self-education" and that the "new satisfactions open to him are largely those of discovery" (p. 299), one teacher explained that Classroom Assessment provides "more challenge, more satisfaction," and another added: "It makes me so much more conscious of what is going on."

Faculty value a teaching community. The efforts of reflective practitioners, teachers in particular, are strengthened by the mutual support gained from working with one another (Schön, 1983). Eight out of the nine faculty at the three community colleges cited the opportunity for collegial interaction during meetings of Classroom Assessment groups with other faculty committed to teaching as a major reward of the practice. This supports Angelo and Cross's (1993) finding that collegiality was one of the most frequently cited benefits of Classroom Assessment. A psychology instructor commented that the Classroom Assessment group prevented "tunnel vision," and a science instructor noted that changes in teaching resulted not only from feedback from CATs, but from "hearing about how people deal with issues that are general to all courses across the disciplines."

Research Findings: Classroom Assessment and Student Learning

As with faculty effects, the research showed advantages and disadvantages for the students.

Advantages of Classroom Assessment for Students. According to faculty, a major benefit of Classroom Assessment to students is *increased control and voice in the classroom*. One faculty survey respondent wrote that "CATs provide students control of the class—a stake in the outcome." Student survey responses supported the faculty perception that students had increased input in the classroom. Over 85 percent of the students surveyed believed that their instructors were "always" or "often" interested in hearing students' concerns or suggestions about the class, and 84 percent indicated that their instructors always or often responded to student concerns and suggestions about the class. A related and very clear finding of this research is that Classroom Assessment increases student satisfaction.

Students responded positively—and with surprise in some cases—to the opportunity to voice their opinions and to help control the organization of the classroom. Students were especially appreciative when faculty made changes in their teaching or the classroom format based on student comments. As one student noted, "She asked you to write down what you liked most and least in the class, which I thought was very good, because she did make a couple of attempts to change her teaching style. . . . She actually started writing a few things on the board near the end. . . . I was impressed."

A second benefit to students, reported by faculty, was that *students are more involved in their own learning* when teachers use Classroom Assessment. In one effort to measure levels of involvement, students were asked to rate how involved they felt in these classes as compared to other college classes. Close to 40 percent reported feeling "more" or "much more" involved in the classes that used Classroom Assessment.

A third advantage of Classroom Assessment to students is that *students benefit from improved teaching* because faculty use "feedback (from CATs) to improve instruction" and that the use of CATs conveys to students "that the instructor cares about them and wants to be effective." When asked to rate their instructors, 64 percent rated their teachers as "above average" or "well above average" in effectiveness. In addition, over half of the students indicated that they were "more" or "much more" satisfied with the classes using CATs than with other classes at the college. Of course, it was not possible to conclude whether teachers are rated as above average because they use CATs, or if teachers who use CATs are highly effective to begin with, but in either case, students were highly satisfied with instruction in courses where teachers used Classroom Assessment.

The final major benefit to Classroom Assessment for students, as reported by faculty, was *increased metacognition and improved ability to monitor their own progress.* Faculty also believed that the use of several CATs forced students to synthesize their learning of new course content or to reflect on their study methods. However, student interview data indicated that students were unaware of teachers' efforts to teach them about learning along with course content. Thus it appeared that faculty were not explicit enough in their efforts to convey how CATs could help students improve their learning and develop new learning strategies. This will be discussed in more detail later.

Disadvantages of Classroom Assessment for Students. In survey and interview data from this study, I rarely found examples of disadvantages of Classroom Assessment for students. In response to an open-ended faculty survey question on this, 20 percent of respondents left the item blank, and nearly 40 percent wrote "none." Faculty reported only two disadvantages of Classroom Assessment to students. The first disadvantage, also mentioned as a disadvantage to faculty, was the *classroom time used and interruption caused* by Classroom Assessment. Faculty were also concerned that some students perceive Classroom Assessment activities as a waste of their time since they generally do not receive grades or course credit for their participation.

One survey respondent commented that Classroom Assessment does "take time away from the learning process, but it is time well spent." Other survey and interview responses, however, suggest that student participation in CATs is not separate from the "learning process"—it contributes to the learning process by encouraging students to reflect on course content and their own understanding of it.

The second disadvantage of Classroom Assessment for students is that it *requires active participation* on the part of students who may prefer to remain passive in the classroom. The ironic tone of faculty comments on forced student involvement—such as "they might feel forced to get involved, you can't sleep all the time"—suggested that students might find getting involved a disadvantage, but faculty believed that students would actually benefit.

Although I did not ask students a specific question about the disadvantages of Classroom Assessment to learners, an analysis of their responses to other questions about their classes and instructors did not yield any comments about wasted time, forced involvement, or any other disadvantages of CATs. The only negative student comments about Classroom Assessment were about teachers who didn't respond to student feedback, and in one instance, a teacher who "bites your head off" after receiving negative feedback on an assessment technique.

Using Classroom Assessment to Promote Metacognition and the Use of Learning Strategies

As mentioned earlier, faculty reported that a key benefit of Classroom Assessment for students was improved metacognition and the ability to monitor their own learning. To measure any beginning-to-end-of-semester changes in students' self-reported use of learning strategies, I used the Motivated Strategies for Learning Questionnaire (MSLQ), a modular instrument with a variety of scales that can be combined according to the needs of the researcher (Pintrich, Smith, Garcia, and McKeachie, 1991). The MSLQ scales used in the pre- and post-test student surveys for this research were Rehearsal Strategies (study techniques for memorization), Elaboration Strategies (study techniques such as paraphrasing and making connections to existing knowledge), Organization Strategies (study techniques such as outlining and determining main points), Metacognitive Strategies (students' reflection on their own learning), and Peer Learning (how often students work with others).

Pre- to post-test scores for the student sample increased on the rehearsal and peer learning scales, but the changes were negligible for all other scales. The only statistically significant difference was found for the rehearsal strategies scale. One possible explanation for the significant increase in student scores on the rehearsal scales is that the survey was administered just before final exams. If exam format requires memorization, then it is logical that students would be using rehearsal strategies. The absence of statistically significant changes for four of the five learning strategy scales could mean that the MSLQ instrument may not be sensitive enough to reflect changes over this short time span, or simply that students did not increase their use of learning strategies during the semester.

The key lesson learned from interview, survey, and MSLQ data is to *be explicit when using CATs to promote student learning.* Helping students learn how to learn requires extra effort on the part of faculty. Teachers may wish to use CATs as a pedagogical tool to embed learning skills instruction into their teaching of course content.

Are faculty currently using Classroom Assessment as a tool to promote student learning skills? In this study, faculty reported that they believed that the activity of participating in CATs and getting feedback from CAT results in itself makes students aware of their learning behaviors and helps them monitor their progress. Based on interviews and classroom observations, it appears that faculty did use CATs such as documented problem set solutions (Angelo and Cross, 1993, p. 222) and student-generated test questions (p. 240) in an effort to help students improve their learning skills by requiring them to monitor, synthesize, organize, and reflect on new material. However, according to interviews with students, faculty did not clarify how the learning behaviors used in CATs could be transferred to other learning and study situations. Consequently, teachers' efforts to improve students' learning skills went unrecognized by students, who were unable to make the connection themselves.

Faculty interview comments suggested that they assumed that simply exposing students to CATs that model new learning strategies would result in improved student learning skills. However, research has indicated that students have a difficult time transferring learning skills from training situations to other tasks (Sternberg, 1983). Unless faculty explain how students might apply and expand upon learning strategies introduced through CATs, such as synthesis in the one sentence summary (Angelo and Cross, 1993, p. 183), reflection in the minute paper, or organization in the concept map (Angelo and Cross, 1993, p. 197), it is unlikely that students will transfer these strategies to their individual study repertoires. For Classroom Assessment to achieve its full potential for improving learning, teachers must be very explicit in their efforts to help students learn about learning.

Recommendations: New Directions for Classroom Assessment Training

Faculty in this study expressed high levels of satisfaction with the outcomes of Classroom Assessment for themselves and their students. Student reports were consistent with their teachers' comments. While faculty have developed skillful approaches for using Classroom Assessment, they still have room to expand that use, especially as a tool to improve students' learning processes. Few faculty know much about theories of learning or approaches to help students transfer what they have learned about learning to other study activities. What follows are some suggestions for going beyond the basic uses of CATs into a deeper understanding and more sophisticated way of thinking about learning.

1. *Faculty need more opportunities to come together and talk about teaching.* Administrators interested in encouraging reflective practice among faculty members should create ongoing opportunities for faculty to come together to talk about teaching. This could be in the form of discussion groups or Classroom Assessment projects that last the entire semester and beyond. Whatever instructional issues faculty choose to focus on, the time will be well spent.

2. *Faculty need more explicit training on the relationship between CATs and cognitive learning theory.* In the same way that faculty need to be explicit to students about the potential applications of CATs to their study strategies, those who conduct CAT workshops for faculty need to be more explicit in pointing out the relationship between CATs and cognitive learning theory. This can involve tapping the resources of both *Classroom Assessment Techniques: A Handbook for College Teachers* (Angelo and Cross, 1993) and *Classroom Research: Implementing the Scholarship of Teaching* (Cross and Steadman, 1996). Both books discuss the theoretical bases for CATs and are designed so that they can be used by individual teachers or collaborative faculty groups. Faculty can engage in activities that cause them to examine the theory behind their favorite CAT or to design learning activities to follow up on the use of CATs in class so that students make the learning connections.

3. *Teachers should consider some key questions about their purposes for using Classroom Assessment.* At the beginning of this chapter, I noted that faculty purposes for using Classroom Assessment influenced how they implemented CATs, what changes they made in their teaching, and how they perceived the impact on their students and teaching. The following questions may help faculty be reflective practitioners as they consider using Classroom Assessment.

Purpose for Using CATs	*Questions to Consider About Potential CATs*
To obtain feedback on teaching and classroom activities	What do I expect to learn about my teaching? What teaching practices or classroom activities do I need feedback on?
To improve teaching	What skills am I interested in improving? How will I use feedback to make changes in my teaching?
To monitor student learning	What will I learn about student comprehension? Will I have to change my presentation format or review material based on CAT results?
To improve communication and collaboration with students	How does this CAT offer students a voice and a stake in controlling the class?
To improve student learning	What is my definition of improved student learning? What will students learn about their learning from this CAT? Does this CAT model any learning strategies?

Facilitators of Classroom Assessment training may also wish to raise these questions with the group. These questions may be especially useful when integrated with information about learning theory to help faculty develop their own connections between improving teaching and improving learning.

Many college campuses have already provided excellent introductory workshops in Classroom Assessment. Now experienced users of Classroom Assessment who desire additional challenges—and new users particularly interested in improving student learning—make up the target audience for enriched and extended Classroom Assessment workshops or advanced Classroom Assessment and Classroom Research faculty groups. These settings support teachers' efforts to apply what is known from research about learning to classroom practice, and to use Classroom Assessment to its fullest potential. The challenge for each institution is how it might adapt and apply some of these ideas to create a Classroom Assessment community on its own campus.

References

Angelo, T. A. *Classroom Research: Early Lessons from Success.* New Directions for Teaching and Learning, no. 46. San Francisco: Jossey-Bass, 1991.

Angelo, T. A., and Cross, K. P. *Classroom Assessment Techniques: A Handbook for College Teachers.* (2nd ed.) San Francisco: Jossey-Bass, 1993.

Carnegie Foundation for the Advancement of Teaching. *The Condition of the Professoriate: Attitudes and Trends, 1989.* Princeton, N.J.: Carnegie Foundation for the Advancement of Teaching, 1989.

Catlin, A., and Kalina, M. *What Is the Effect of the Cross/Angelo Model of Classroom Assessment on Student Outcome? A Study of the Classroom Assessment Project at Eight California Community Colleges.* Research project funded by the California Community College Chancellor's Office, Funds for Instructional Improvement Grant 92–0016, 1993.

Cross, K. P., and Angelo, T. A. *Classroom Assessment Techniques: A Handbook for Faculty.* Ann Arbor, Mich.: National Center for Research to Improve Postsecondary Teaching and Learning, 1988.

Cross, K. P., and Steadman, M. H. *Classroom Research: Implementing the Scholarship of Teaching.* San Francisco: Jossey-Bass, 1996.

Csikszentmihalyi, M. "Intrinsic Motivation and Effective Teaching: A Flow Analysis." In J. L. Bess (ed.) *Motivating Professors to Teach Effectively.* New Directions for Teaching and Learning, no. 10. San Francisco: Jossey-Bass, 1982.

Cuevas, G. J. "Feedback from Classroom Research Projects." *Community-Junior College Quarterly of Research and Practice,* 1991, *15* (4), 381–390.

Frase L. E., and Piland, W. E. "Breaking the Silence About Faculty Rewards." *Community College Review,* 1989, *17* (1), 25–33.

Kelly, D. K. *Classroom Research and Interactive Learning: Assessing the Impact on Adult Learners and Faculty.* Unpublished doctoral dissertation, Claremont Graduate School, Claremont, Calif., 1993. (Order Number DA 9330348)

Kozma, R. B. "Communication, Rewards, and the Use of Classroom Innovations." *Journal of Higher Education,* 1979, *50* (6), 761–771.

Pintrich, P. R., Smith, D.A.F., Garcia, T., and McKeachie, W. J. *A Manual for the Use of the Motivated Strategies for Learning Questionnaire.* (Tech. Report No. 91–B–004). Ann Arbor: Regents of the University of Michigan, School of Education, National Center for Research to Improve Postsecondary Teaching and Learning, 1991.

Rogers, E. M. *Diffusion of Innovations.* (3rd ed.) New York: Free Press, 1983.

Schön, D. A. *The Reflective Practitioner: How Professionals Think in Action.* New York: Basic Books, 1983.

Steadman, M. H. *CATs for Community Colleges: Changing Both Sides of the Teaching and Learning Equation.* Executive Summary of Practitioner-Based Research Project, Saratoga Springs, N.Y.: National Center on Adult Learning, Empire State College, 1994a.

Steadman, M. H. *Implementation and Impact of Classroom Assessment Techniques in Community Colleges.* Unpublished doctoral dissertation, University of California, Berkeley, 1994b. (UMI Microform no. 9528688)

Sternberg, R. J. "Criteria for Intellectual Skills Training." *Educational Researcher,* 1983, *12,* 6–12.

MIMI STEADMAN *is a private consultant on Classroom Assessment and Classroom Research operating out of New York.*

This chapter describes how two classroom researchers used CATs to study learning.

Do Classroom Assessment Techniques (CATs) Improve Student Learning?

Philip Cottell, Elaine Harwood

For years accounting students were taught, primarily by lecture and example, to memorize the technical aspects of accounting and use their knowledge to find correct answers to accounting problems. This worked well until the business world became more dynamic and complex, and it not only became difficult to memorize the rapidly growing body of accounting knowledge, it grew tougher to find a "correct" answer to the complex issues accounting professionals faced. The skills students needed to enter the profession were changing, placing greater emphasis on professional judgment, communication skills, interpersonal skills, and the ability to use technology effectively, but accounting education didn't keep up (see Williams, 1993).

A little over a decade ago, the gap between the skills graduates needed and those accounting programs developed became big enough to lead to a call for change by both practicing accountants and accounting academics (American Accounting Association, 1986; Arthur Andersen and others, 1989). To promote the types of changes that were needed, and to do so quickly, the largest CPA firms joined together with the largest professional organization of accounting academics—the American Accounting Association (AAA)—to form the Accounting Education Change Commission (AECC). The AECC provided grants for curriculum development, issued statements that tackled critical issues surrounding teaching philosophy and pedagogy, and supported workshops and publications, all to improve what students learned from their accounting programs.

With its focus on student learning, the AECC became a "driving force" that increased attention on and the demand for assessment (Williams, 1997). It provided workshops on assessment, encouraged schools that received grants to put assessment programs in place, and funded a comprehensive guide for developing assessment programs (Gainen and Locatelli, 1995).

It may be because our discipline has been so actively involved in evaluating the things we can do to improve learning, or it may just be part of our accounting nature, but when we started working with Classroom Assessment Techniques (CATs) we became curious about the bottom line. In other words, we wanted to know if the benefits of assessment exceeded the costs. From the perspective of accounting educators, CATs provided valuable feedback to make important course planning decisions and changes to improve learning and seemed to motivate students to become more active learners (Cottell, 1991; Beard, 1993; Cohen and Kugel, 1994; Harwood, 1998). But we recognized that a full accounting for the costs and benefits meant that we needed to consider not only the perspective of professors but the perspective of students as well. We decided to conduct an experiment to test whether there is a positive bottom line—that is, whether we could use CATs to improve what students learned in our classes.

Model and Hypothesis Development

With the recent challenges to accounting education in mind, Frederickson and Pratt (1995) developed a model of the education process. In their model, designed to address accounting at the program level, the objective is to minimize the difference between the competencies employers demand and the competencies graduates possess. Educators meet that objective by varying several decision parameters—admission policies, curriculum, course content, and instructional methods—within the constraints imposed by faculty, students, and the academic institution.

By bringing this model to the single-class setting we can better understand how using one specific instructional method, CATs, can improve student learning. This understanding can help us design a more powerful experiment of the learning effects of CATs.

Our model is depicted in Figure 4.1. Students start the class with a set of competencies, a level of individual ability, and an attitude toward and motivation for the subject. They learn by developing a set of revised competencies, which they carry forward—together with their ability, attitude, and motivation—as they move through their accounting program. If the learning process is successful, the revised set of competencies moves the student closer to the competencies ultimately demanded by future employers.

What happens between the beginning and ending competencies occurs in an environment that depends on other students and the professor. The professor uses his or her talents to design an effective course with the learning needs of the students in mind, setting explicit goals and objectives for the class and developing a learning plan to achieve those goals. During the planning process the professor makes numerous assumptions about the students, and many of these assumptions can be tested by using CATs throughout the class term.

Figure 4.1 Model of the Learning Process

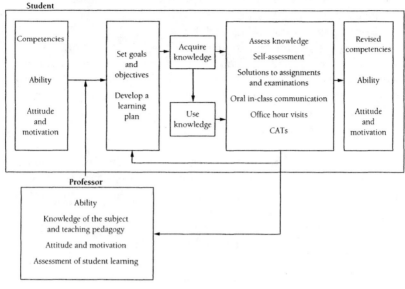

Student

Competencies	Set goals and objectives	Acquire knowledge	Assess knowledge	Revised competencies
Ability			Self-assessment	Ability
			Solutions to assignments and examinations	
Attitude and motivation	Develop a learning plan	Use knowledge	Oral in-class communication	Attitude and motivation
			Office hour visits	
			CATs	

Professor

Ability

Knowledge of the subject
and teaching pedagogy

Attitude and motivation

Assessment of student learning

Learning Environment

How well the student learns the material will be influenced, in part, by the degree to which the student internalizes the professor's goals, objectives, and plans for the course. In addition to general goals for the class, both the professor and student approach each topic with goals, objectives, and a learning plan that motivate and guide the student through the acquisition and use of knowledge. The process is a dynamic, ongoing sequence of acquiring, using, and assessing knowledge.

Students acquire knowledge in the form of facts, terms, concepts, and problem-solving approaches. This phase of learning generally begins with reading course materials or listening to a lecture. The student, to some degree, assesses the knowledge gained. Based on the assessment, the student either revises his or her competencies or decides to go back, with an objective of improved understanding, to look at the material again. Consistent with a hierarchy of learning (Bloom and others, 1956), some form of knowledge acquisition and comprehension needs to happen before knowledge can be used.

In a typical accounting class, professors require students to use their knowledge to solve problems. In the problem-solving context, students naturally look for feedback to assess learning. For example, students completing a homework problem compare their answers to the solutions manual. Based on an assessment of their knowledge the students either revise their competencies or set an objective of understanding where the problem-solving process went wrong and decide to return to acquire the knowledge they need.

The professor plays a guiding role in this ongoing process of student learning. A large amount of what the professor does in a class as well as what students are encouraged to do can be changed in response to student learning needs. Making those changes requires a professor to decide why, how, and when the changes should be made. These decisions can be addressed using feedback from assessment, as Figure 4.1 shows.

In classes where professors do not use CATs, the professor typically relies on feedback from written assignments, examinations, and oral communication in class and during office hours. CATs offer a valuable supplement to these traditional approaches because they are formative and based on an ongoing student-professor feedback loop. Thus professors can improve student learning by using the feedback from CATs to exercise greater discretion over when and how to make midcourse adjustments. But this feedback comes at a cost, most frequently related to time, class coverage, and closure (Angelo, 1991). When the benefits of CATs exceed their costs, students should learn more in classes where they use them. This is the general research hypothesis we are interested in testing.

We use three measures of learning to test this hypothesis. First, we use the grades students earn, taking care to link assignments and exams to specific learning objectives and to develop grading keys that assign points based on achieving those objectives. Second, we use student participation to explore whether, as Angelo and Cross (1993) suggest and our colleagues have experienced, students who assess their own learning become more motivated to take an active role in it. Third, we use students' perceptions of their learning—on the basis that if CATs improved students' self-awareness of learning, as suggested by Angelo and Cross, they should have a favorable effect on students' perceptions of what they learn.

As discussed in the following section, we selected CATs that emphasized study skills and problem-solving skills through application, performance, analysis, and critical thinking. We further adapted each CAT to the technical course material. We then measured students' perceptions of their learning of study skills, problem-solving skills, and technical material.

Research Design

The recent focus on improving learning in accounting classes has meant that professors tend to make more changes to their classes from one semester to the next than they did in quieter times. While these changes may include using CATs, only a limited number of accounting professors have extensive experience with Classroom Assessment. Our research design reflects these discipline-specific factors, being based on one semester of classes taught by two professors. With this design, we faced three important issues of selecting the treatment and control groups, deciding how to handle midcourse adjustments, and choosing CATs for the treatment group.

Selecting the Treatment and Control Groups. Each professor taught two classes covering the same subject, with one class immediately following the other. Professors often think there's a "second class" effect, meaning the second class tends to go better than the first. Maybe professors are making quick adjustments based on listening to student questions, observing their body language or just getting a feel for how the first class went. In our experience, the second class effect seems to be related to the amount of time we spend directing class activities, being more pronounced for lecture-based classes.

Our teaching styles and the nature of the courses we taught meant that we planned classes that would actively involve students in learning through cooperative learning exercises and cases. Regardless, we did not want a potential second class effect to bias the study in favor of finding significant improvements in learning, so we selected the first class as the treatment group and the second as the control.

Deciding How to Handle Midcourse Adjustments. We realized that the students in classes using CATs would give us valuable information that we could use to improve teaching and learning. How could we ignore that information for control class students?

To deal with this dilemma, we thought about the types of changes we make based on the information CATs provide. We were able to isolate two types. The first type, which we'll call "specific," prompts the professor or student to make detailed, discrete, and often temporary changes in behavior. For example, a professor may review a tricky aspect of pension accounting because students wrote questions about it on a minute paper. The second type, which we'll call "general," prompts the professor or student to make broad, sweeping, and typically lasting changes in behavior. For example, a professor may allocate more class time to lecture based on a suggestion from the quality control circle.

When we thought about these types of changes we realized that we would only feel uncomfortable if we didn't make the general changes for both classes. We decided to go ahead and make those changes, even though we realized we introduced a bias against finding the result that CATs improved learning. After all, even without the general changes made by the professor, the treatment group would benefit from the specific changes the professors made and the general and specific changes that the students made as well. As it turned out, we did not make many general changes for both classes.

Choosing CATs for the Treatment Group. Harwood (1998) found that accounting students valued one CAT that they used repeatedly throughout the semester. While we recognized that her study stopped short of measuring student learning, we felt we needed research that considered the effects of using several different CATs.

When choosing CATs for our classes, we benefited not only from the selection provided by Angelo and Cross (1993), but the classification they provided as well. As shown in Table 4.1, we selected CATs from many of their assessment categories. We used each CAT at least twice, generally once a week.

We selected a variety of CATs to assess different aspects of student learning for a number of reasons. This approach allowed us to get an overview of students' general strengths and weaknesses, while giving us a chance to look

Table 4.1. Classroom Assessment Techniques (CATs) Used

Area Assessed by the CAT	CATs Used
Prior knowledge, recall, and understanding	Background knowledge probe, minute paper, feedback form
Skill in applications and performance	Directed paraphrasing
Skill in analysis and critical thinking	Pro and con grid
Course-related learning and study skills	What did I learn from the exam?
Learner reaction to teachers and teaching	Classroom assessment quality circle group instructional feedback technique
Learner reaction to class activities, assignments, and materials	Group-work evaluation form

Note: Angelo and Cross (1993) provide an overview and examples of these CATs—except for the feedback form, which is introduced in Harwood (1998). "What did I learn from the exam?" is very similar to the "Homework Assignment and Test Entry" portion of the Diagnostic Learning Log found in Angelo and Cross (1993, p. 313).

at specific aspects of learning such as students' abilities to work well in groups. This appealed to us because we knew our classes required a diverse set of skills in students and we did not know of one particular skill we wanted to improve in all students. In fact, we thought students could use this variety of CATs to survey their own learning and target specific areas in which they felt the need to improve.

Results

The research hypothesis asks whether CATs improve student learning. In terms of the model of the learning process diagrammed in Figure 4.1, improved learning means that although students may start the class with relatively similar competencies, those in CATs classes should develop a set of revised competencies superior to those in the control classes. We checked to see if students started the class with similar beginning competencies by comparing their self-reported GPAs and found no significant differences.

To the extent grades measure the competencies students develop during the semester, we can use them to see whether CATs improved learning. Table 4.2 shows the average grades given to students in CATs and control classes, along with detailed information about examinations, group work, and class contribution.

There aren't many significant differences in the distributions of grades reported in Table 4.2. Interestingly, at each university one class seemed to dominate the other, typically earning slightly higher grades on nearly every course element. Because the dominant class was the CATs class at University A and the

Table 4.2. Comparison of Grade Distributions

	University A			University B		
	CATs class	Control class	t stat. p value	CATs class	Control class	t stat. p value
Number of students	47	35	n.a.	26	22	n.a.
Course grade	3.17	3.12	0.27	2.72	2.94	−0.85
	(0.86)	(0.66)	p = 0.79	(0.89)	(0.90)	p = 0.40
Examinations:						
Exam 1	85.23%	86.46%	−0.94	77.88%	80.77%	−0.62
	(0.06)	(0.05)	p = 0.35	(0.18)	(0.13)	p = 0.54
Exam 2	81.91%	80.66%	0.33	62.46%	67.39%	−1.32
	(0.17)	(0.16)	p = 0.74	(0.13)	(0.12)	p = 0.19
Group work:						
Group project	88.44%	87.94%	0.54			
	(0.05)	(0.03)	p = 0.59			
Team learning quizzes				75.00%	74.09%	0.37
				(0.06)	(0.11)	p = 0.72
In-class group problems			77.51%	84.21%	−4.10	
				(0.06)	(0.05)	p = 0.00
Contribution:						
Class contribution	86.02%	81.30%	1.57			
	(0.14)	(0.13)	p = 0.12			

Note: This table provides information on the distribution of course grades and specific components of those grades, comparing CATs to control classes. Average grades are reported with standard deviations in parentheses. Reported *p* values are based on two-tailed tests.

control class at University B, these results do not suggest that CATs systematically played a role in student learning as measured by graded course elements.

Although contribution was only used for grading purposes at one university, both professors tracked in-class participation, including when students asked questions, responded to questions raised by the professor, or participated in class discussion. (See Cottell and Harwood, 1998, for a detailed discussion of the measurement of participation and a graph showing the trends in participation for CATs and control classes.) The patterns of participation between the CATs and control classes were extremely variable. The control classes began the semester with a higher level of participation than the CATs classes, but the differences disappeared in the second half of the semester. It is difficult to say if the use of specific CATs led to the change, but both professors used group work evaluations and the group instructional feedback technique during that period. If changes in participation were related to those CATs, the effects were not enduring. Participation in the last quarter of the class was highly variable in both CATs and control classes. Given this data, we could not conclude that using CATs had a systematic effect on the number of students who participated in class.

At the end of the semester we surveyed students to find out if the CATs students perceived that they learned more than the control students. In addition to asking students their expected grade, we asked the degree to which they thought they learned study skills, problem-solving skills, and the technical material. A comparison of their responses is provided in Table 4.3. Although students' perceptions were not significantly different, Table 4.3 shows that the control students, rather than the CATs students, tended to feel that they learned slightly more.

We considered students' perceptions to be an important part of our analysis because many of the factors that could affect student learning, diagrammed in Figure 4.1, are based on students' perceptions. To find out about one factor that could affect learning, CATs, we needed to remove the influence of the other factors. We did this by running a regression model that included a variable to capture the difference between CATs and control class students along with variables that controlled for students' beginning competencies, ability, attitude and motivation, effort, and other aspects of the learning environment. Given the results in Table 4.3, we were not too surprised that we did not find CATs to be an important factor in explaining students' perceptions of their learning.

Concluding Remarks

Significant changes in accounting education motivated us to take a look at the benefits and costs of using CATs to improve student learning. Based on a study that concentrated on students and was built around a model of the learning process, we found a bottom line that suggested no gain or loss from using CATs.

As accounting educators, we are accustomed to teaching students that even though the bottom line provides an important summary of what happened, there is much to be learned by looking at the details that led to that end result. Following our own advice, we took a closer look at the costs and benefits for students in this study.

Table 4.3. Comparison of Student Perceptions of What They Learned

	CATs Classes	Control Classes	t stat. p value
Number of students	52	42	n.a.
Expected grade	3.21 (0.51)	3.23 (0.50)	0.24 p = 0.81
Learned study skills	3.33 (0.96)	3.40 (0.94)	0.39 p = 0.69
Learned problem-solving skills	3.46 (0.87)	3.50 (0.83)	0.22 p = 0.83
Learned technical material	4.13 (0.49)	4.02 (0.68)	−0.89 p = 0.38

Note: This table provides information on the distributions of students' perceptions of their expected grade and of what they learned, comparing CATs to control classes. Averages are reported with standard deviations in parentheses. Reported p values are based on two-tailed tests.

With respect to costs, we collected data to measure students' perceptions of the most frequently cited costs of time, class coverage, and closure (Angelo, 1991). We were surprised that more students in CATs classes than control students agreed with the statement "Class time was adequate to cover all of the material." The same thing happened when we asked students about closure—more CATs students agreed that the professor answered their questions well.

Because the data suggested that costs were not driving our results, we thought about whether there was something that had kept students from getting the most benefit from CATs. An aspect of our research design such as making general midcourse adjustments to both classes could have decreased the relative benefits for CATs students. Or students may need to develop a routine of assessment, which we may not have accomplished because we asked them to use many different CATs. Future research is needed to test these potential explanations so that we can better understand whether CATs can improve student learning.

Rather than disheartening us about the usefulness of CATs, the results of this research support the notion that such strategies involve a complex mix of the variables identified in Figure 4.1. Future research needs to focus more on the role CATs play in the process of learning, particularly focusing on what makes the feedback from CATs useful and what inhibits its usefulness. We hope this study motivates others to take a closer look at these issues.

References

American Accounting Association, Committee on the Future Structure. "Content and Scope of Accounting Education. Future Accounting Education: Preparing for the Expanding Profession." *Issues in Accounting Education,* Spring 1986, pp. 168–195.

Angelo, T. A. "Introduction and Overview: From Classroom Assessment to Classroom Research." In T. A. Angelo (ed.), *Classroom Research: Early Lessons from Success.* New Directions for Teaching and Learning, no. 46. San Francisco: Jossey-Bass, 1991.

Angelo, T. A., and Cross, K. P. *Classroom Assessment Techniques: A Handbook for College Teachers.* (2nd ed.) San Francisco: Jossey-Bass, 1993.

Arthur Andersen & Co., Ernst & Whitney, Arthur Young, Peat Marwick Main & Co., Coopers & Lybrand, Price Waterhouse, Deloitte Haskins & Sells, and Touche Ross. "Perspectives on Education: Capabilities for Success in the Accounting Profession." Perspectives Paper. 1989.

Beard, V. "Classroom Assessment Techniques (CATs): Tools for Improving Accounting Education." *Journal of Accounting Education,* 1993, *11,* 293–300.

Bloom, B. S., Engelhart, M., Furst, E., Hill, W., and Krathwohl, D. *Taxonomy of Educational Objectives: The Classification of Educational Goals. Handbook 1, Cognitive Domain.* New York: McKay, 1956.

Cohen, J., and Kugel, P. "The Class Committee and Other Recipes for Gourmet Teaching." *College Teaching,* Summer 1994, p. 82.

Cottell, P. G., Jr. "Classroom Research in Accounting: Assessing for Learning." In T. A. Angelo (ed.), *Classroom Research: Early Lessons from Success.* New Directions for Teaching and Learning, no. 46. San Francisco: Jossey-Bass, 1991.

Cottell, P. G., Jr., and Harwood, E. "Do Classroom Assessment Techniques (CATs) Improve Student Learning?" Working Paper, Boston College, 1998.

Frederickson, J. R., and Pratt, J. "A Model of the Accounting Education Process." *Issues in Accounting Education,* 1995, *10* (2), 229–246.

Gainen, J., and Locatelli, P. *Assessment for the New Curriculum: A Guide for Professional Accounting Programs.* Sarasota, Fla.: American Accounting Association, 1995.

Harwood, E. "Student Perceptions of the Effects of Classroom Assessment Techniques (CATs)." Working Paper, Boston College, 1998.

Williams, D. Z. "Reforming Accounting Education." *Journal of Accountancy.* Aug. 1993, pp. 76–82.

Williams, D. Z. "College of Business Perspective." Presentation at the AECC/Notre Dame Assessment Conference, Measuring the Path of Excellence: What Works Well in Accounting Education, May 29, 1997.

PHILIP COTTELL *is professor of accounting at Miami University.*

ELAINE HARWOOD *is assistant professor of accounting at Boston College.*

Classroom Assessment may be a good complement to the quality movement.

Quality in the Classroom: Classroom Assessment Techniques as TQM

Elaine Soetaert

Higher education, under ever-increasing pressure to serve more students, provide high-quality instruction, and produce highly skilled graduates—all with less and less money—is beginning to explore total quality management (TQM) and the analogous continuous quality improvement (CQI) as possible answers to the dilemma (Bogue and Saunders, 1992). The Classroom Assessment Techniques (CATs) developed by Angelo and Cross (1993) are designed to provide feedback to an instructor about what is, and what is not, being learned in the classroom. For that reason, the techniques allow the instructor to gather "profound knowledge" (Deming, 1986) about which processes are having a positive result on learning and which need improvement. "The purpose of classroom research is to improve the quality of learning in college classrooms by improving the effectiveness of teaching" (Cross and Angelo, 1989). El Camino College in California reports that "the alliance of the Classroom Assessment Technique with the philosophy of continuous quality improvement . . . has finally provided a focus and a forum for the application of TQM principles and practices directly in the classroom" (Schauerman and Peachy, 1993, p. 8).

The Question

Finding appropriate ways to incorporate CQI and TQM in the classroom is a challenge that educational institutions are presently attempting to address. In the fall of 1995, the study described in this chapter was conducted to explore faculty and student perceptions of the effectiveness of the use of the Cross-Angelo CATs as a method of improving the quality of the teaching and learning

New Directions for Teaching and Learning, no. 75, Fall 1998 © Jossey-Bass Publishers process in a postsecondary technical institution that was in its infancy in adopt-ing and applying the quality principles.

The Study

Ten instructors volunteered for participation in the study and were trained in CATs. They represented experience ranging from one year to more than ten years and a wide variety of programs. The participating faculty were requested to use CATs in a class of their choice at least five times during the semester and to meet bimonthly with other faculty in a support group. In addition, faculty and the stu-dents in their selected classes responded to surveys about their impressions of the use of CATs. Faculty also responded to an open-ended questionnaire that allowed more specific questions about their experiences with CATs.

Faculty Results. When instructors were asked "In your opinion, did the use of CATs improve the quality of teaching and learning in your class?" every instructor replied with a resounding yes. The results of the closed-ended sur-vey showed that faculty found the use of CATs helpful and not intrusive, and most planned to use the techniques again in other classes. Table 5.1 summa-rizes faculty responses to the survey.

To the open-ended questions, faculty identified four areas where they felt CATs had been particularly helpful. The first of these was *student learning*. When using CATs that focused on student learning, the instructors felt they could identify concepts that were unclear, confused, or missed completely. Instructor comments included, "The muddiest point CAT, for example, allowed us to go back and clear up areas where students were struggling" and "The self-confidence survey told [showed] me that I forgot to teach a skill."

CATs were used by some instructors to sense students' response to *the process of instruction*. One instructor commented, "At the start of the semester, I was going too fast, I didn't realize how much the materials would need to be broken down. The CATs made it clear which areas needed to be emphasized." CATs that focus on process were used to monitor new instructional strategies. One instructor replied to a question on whether CATs improved class quality, "Yes, especially with respect to the new process of coop[erative] learning."

Instructors recognized the effect the use of CATs had on *the classroom envi-ronment* for learning. They felt it improved the quality of the student learning experience. As one participant noted, "Students felt their opinion was valued and important, therefore increased commitment to being in class and being successful."

Classroom Assessment was used to *promote student cognition* by enabling the students to organize concepts and clarify their thinking about those con-cepts. One instructor stated, "They [the CATs] helped students to consolidate information (minute paper/pros-cons) and reflect on their experiences and strengths (assignment assessment/self-confidence survey)."

Student Results. Students also strongly endorsed the use of CATS as a method for enhancing the quality of their learning. Over 75 percent of students

Table 5.1. Faculty Responses to Closed-Ended Items

Statement	Strongly agree	Agree	Disagree	Strongly disagree
The use of CATs in my classroom contributed to an improvement in the teaching and learning process.	3	7	0	0
The use of CATs was difficult for me.	0	1	6	2
CATs are easy tools to use.	4	5	1	0
The use of CATs is a time-consuming process.	1	2	7	0
I will use CATs again.	6	4	0	0
I plan to introduce CATs to all my classes.	3	6	1	0
I would recommend the use of CATs to a colleague.	3	7	0	0
The use of CATs made me feel more effective in the classroom.	4	5	1	0
I enjoyed the sharing of information with my colleagues in our CATs meetings.	4	6	0	0
I feel more excited about my teaching since I have started using CATs.	3	4	3	0
In my opinion, CATs are effective tools for improving the teaching and learning process.	6	4	0	0

agreed or strongly agreed that the use of CATs in their class improved the quality of their education experience in that class. Students found the time used during class in the gathering and reporting of assessments to be time well spent. Over 86 percent felt that CATs were an important tool to aid in the communication between students and instructors, and 83 percent felt that CATs enabled them to feel more involved in their learning. Students were so impressed with CATs as an instructional communication tool that over 83 percent felt all instructors should use CATs and 88 percent would prefer to be in a class that was using CATs if they had a choice. Table 5.2 presents the student responses to the survey.

This support of the use of CATs by students is an important finding. Students' enthusiasm for the use of CATs as an appropriate means to improve their learning experience provides us with information about the student customers' response to the use of the tools of Classroom Assessment. Although, to my knowledge, this is the first study that directly explores the student customers' response to Classroom Assessment as a CQI tool, Kelly (1993) and Steadman (1994) report similar positive student responses to CATs.

Table 5.2. Student Responses to Survey

Statement	Strongly agree n (%)	Agree n (%)	Disagree n (%)	Strongly Disagree n (%)
Classroom assessment is a waste of time.	3 (1.30)	11 (4.78)	116 (50.43)	98 (42.61)
Classroom assessments allowed me to communicate in a positive way with my instructor.	83 (36.09)	116 (50.43)	24 (10.43)	5 (2.17)
If I had a choice, I would choose to be in a class with an instructor who uses classroom assessments.	92 (40.00)	110 (47.83)	21 (9.13)	4 (1.74)
The use of classroom assessments had little or no effect on my learning.	11 (4.78)	52 (22.61)	126 (54.78)	37 (16.09)
The use of classroom assessments made me feel more involved in my learning.	62 (26.96)	128 (55.65)	30 (13.04)	8 (3.48)
The use of classroom assessments improved the quality of my educational experience in this class.	38 (16.52)	135 (58.70)	44 (19.13)	11 (4.78)
All instructors should use classroom assessments.	87 (37.83)	104 (45.22)	20 (8.70)	7 (3.04)

Recommendations About Classroom Assessment and Quality Improvement

• Teaching circles: *Classroom Assessment and research support groups (teaching circles) should be organized and supported for faculty who are implementing innovations in their classrooms.*

When new techniques are introduced into the classroom, faculty often feel somewhat discomforted by the process due to the technique's unfamiliarity. This may lead to the appearance of being disorganized, unprepared, and tentative even though this is not the case. Students often respond negatively if they perceive that instructors are not clear about what they are doing. In addition, students have clearly formulated expectations of what the teaching and learning process should look like. When first exposed to new techniques such as cooperative learning or Classroom Assessment, students sometimes respond with defensiveness or hostility. These attitudes can cause a valuable teaching tool to be discarded before it has had an opportunity to prove its worth.

With this in mind, faculty need strong support for their attempts to integrate new techniques, new forms of feedback, and efforts to improve the quality of teaching and learning. To gain this support faculty need to seek assistance from various sources that their institution should provide. Kozma (1979) identified factors that influence the adoption and dissemination of classroom innovations in higher education. "These factors include the: (1) informal network (social interaction), (2) formal network (resources and consultants), (3) intrinsic reward (satisfaction derived from the activity), and (4) extrinsic reward (such as the encouragement of administrators)" (Steadman, 1994, p. 205).

Teaching circles—groups of faculty who meet regularly to discuss an aspect of the teaching and learning process—are a very valuable method of using the informal network to support innovation. Through the teaching circle, participants gain a sense of camaraderie and interconnectedness with other faculty. Faculty speak about their experiences, explore relevant literature, and learn from each other.

For example, instructors in this study commented on the need for CAT questions to be very specific. General questions did not reveal elements that could be improved upon. One of the best ways for instructors to get help in framing good questions was through their teaching circles. Colleagues reviewed questions before they went to the students and helped to frame them in a more useable way.

It is of primary importance that the teaching circles or support groups connote a positive image (Berry, Filbeck, Rothstein-Fisch, and Saltman, 1991). No one is interested in joining an activity that hints at being aimed at a group of ineffective teachers in need of help. Choosing a positive name for the activity, perhaps Classroom Research Group or Classroom Assessment Group, would connote a positive image.

• Student learning focus: *Instructors should be supported and encouraged to move beyond using Classroom Assessment to improve instruction to using Classroom Assessment to improve student learning.*

Classroom Assessment is an excellent tool for improving the quality of the teaching and learning situation. While faculty involved in this study were deeply committed to enabling student learning, they had little background in theories of teaching and learning. Most were untrained in approaches to help students transfer what they had learned about learning from their experience with Classroom Assessment to other situations, a common problem in higher education (Steadman, 1994).

To enable transfer of this learning, faculty need to be explicit with students about the potential applications of CATs to varying learning situations. This requires that faculty become familiar with the relationship between CATs and cognitive learning theory. Thus when an institution is embarking on a Classroom Assessment project, the facilitators should help faculty make the connections between CATs and learning theory more explicit. Some examples of how this might be done are described in Chapter 2 of this volume.

Creating connections between CATs and student learning will not suit all faculty. Some faculty, depending on their goals, will use CATs exclusively for feedback on instruction. This recommendation is included to promote a consideration of the expansion of the use of Classroom Assessment beyond that of improvement of instruction to improvement of learning.

• Administrative support: *Administration should formally and informally support the implementation and use of Classroom Assessment.*

Any program of faculty development or CQI requires the visible support of administration for it to succeed. Even though there will always be faculty who pursue development due to the intrinsic motivation of improvement, for a program to succeed campuswide, faculty need to be encouraged to become involved and stay involved over the long term. "Getting people to do not just one thing right, but to adopt the new behavior as a consistent way of working, takes a long time" (Atkinson, 1990, p. 47).

Faculty should seek support from relevant administrators before embarking on their journey of innovation. The practice has a number of benefits. First, administrators cannot offer support and encouragement if they are uninformed about what the instructor is doing. Second, informing administrators of the intent to innovate brings a deeper commitment to follow through when the process gets difficult. Knowing that the administrator will be asking about the innovation can provide motivation to follow through. Third, if students react negatively to the innovation, the administrator is less likely to see student complaints as an indication of poor instruction. Also, if the administrator is the person who has "primary responsibility for evaluating . . . instructional activities . . . he should understand what I [the instructor] was doing and why" (Cottell, 1991, p. 44).

Further, any formal or informal group of faculty involved in innovation could be coordinated through the department on campus that is responsible for faculty development or continuous improvement to tap into the knowledge of the organization (Watkins and Marsick, 1993). This would allow faculty access to training and support as needed. This would incorporate Kozma's (1979) finding that access to training and expert support is one of the four cornerstones of innovative practice.

Results of innovations should be made available to other faculty, possibly by a unit such as a Center for Teaching Excellence. Faculty would then have a resource to refer to when planning further innovations. Certainly there are a large number of published articles and research reports that could be of value to faculty, but reports generated by peers in the same organizational culture are invaluable. This recording, reporting, and subsequent use of information builds a "learning organization" culture (Watkins and Marsick, 1993; Senge, 1990). In addition to the public benefit, the instructor receives a great deal of personal benefit by maintaining a log and submitting reports. The submission of the report makes the instructor publicly accountable for improving teaching and learning. The writing of the report provides an opportunity for personal reflection. The thinking that is involved reinforces the learning experienced and provides an opportunity to analyze the process from a different perspective removed from the "heat of the moment" in the classroom.

The top levels of administration—the president and vice president—need to encourage deans to support programs of Classroom Research throughout their schools. Program or department heads could organize teams of faculty to embark on quality improvement projects using Classroom Research. The importance of such work could be communicated to the faculty by including a category about CQI on annual evaluations. Consideration for the time and effort such improvement takes should be recognized by being taken into account in workloads. A facilitator or team leader should be assigned to organize and support teaching circles and individuals in their work with Classroom Research and quality improvement. This person would need to bring "personal credibility and visibility on issues and concerns of teaching and learning, the authority to promote and reward faculty development efforts, and the capacity to provide necessary funding and administrative support (Berry, Filbeck, Rothstein-Fisch, and Saltman, 1991, p. 94)

Communicating information about successful Classroom Research and classroom quality improvement projects is a mode by which the use of the processes could be celebrated and spread throughout the campus. Reports about successful projects could be included in CQI publications and faculty newsletters.

Cuevas (1991) states:

> If the concept of classroom feedback/research is to be successfully implemented at the community college level, there needs to be an institutional support system to facilitate faculty research activities. This support system may involve:
> • Networks for faculty to assist each other in the development and implementation of assessment strategies
> • Availability of a variety of assessment "tools" which can be readily used or adapted to learning/teaching situations
> • Assistance with data analysis
> • Availability of "model" instructional strategies which faculty can use to follow up assessment results, and
> • Release time for Classroom Research [p. 389].

Assessment tools can be provided by making available the Angelo and Cross text *Classroom Assessment Techniques,* 1993 edition. Indeed, faculty in this study identified access to this text as a requirement for the success of the use of Classroom Assessment. Model instructional strategies and advice on modifying strategies can be gained through faculty support groups and from the reports submitted by instructors to the Center for Teaching Excellence.

Faculty in this study identified administrative support and encouragement as important for the success of their use of Classroom Assessment for the improvement of instruction. It would seem reasonable and necessary to support and reward those people who strive for excellence in their classroom. Cross outlines what administrators can do to improve teaching:

> Classroom Research has its own built-in incentives, because the process itself is intellectually challenging, promotes discussion and recognition across disciplinary and even institutional boundaries, and enhances the status and satisfaction

of teaching. There are, however, many things administrators can do to encourage Classroom Research, including the following:

1. Devise a promotion and tenure system that recognizes teaching performance and efforts to engage in professional activities such as Classroom Research.
2. Provide and support opportunities for teachers to engage in Classroom Research, individually, in small clusters of interested and motivated faculty, and as an important aspect of departmental improvement and evaluation.
3. Provide opportunities for teachers to increase their knowledge base and gain professional recognition through attendance at professional meetings and participation in graduate-level courses or faculty development activities emphasizing the collection and analysis of Classroom Research.
4. Promote local discussions of Classroom Research projects affording teachers an opportunity to share designs and findings and to receive local recognition for participation in growth-enhancing professional development [1990, p. 140].

A Perspective for the Future

Faculty use of CATs improves the quality of students' learning experience. The techniques are appropriate tools for assessing teaching and learning products and processes. Groups of faculty using CATs provide a forum for the investigation of teaching and learning, critical thinking and reflection, and a celebration of high-quality learning and instruction. As faculty get more involved in a process that is intrinsically motivating, they feel revitalized and interested in their classes once again. The culture of the organization begins to change as instructors begin to build their belief system to accommodate the attitude that improvement is not only possible, but also rewarding. Faculty can begin to build "a belief system that spreads hope . . . that results from the act of pursuing personal involvement and sharing power—a feeling of self-determination" (Seymour, 1995, p. 162). "Personal involvement in the classroom, along with the idea that enabling students to influence their environment has a direct effect on [faculty's] willingness and ability to perform, is (an attitude) that is long overdue on most campuses" (Seymour, 1995, p. 168). Students feel more involved in their learning when CATs are being used. The continued use, support, and promotion of Classroom Assessment has the potential to move educational institutions forward on their journey of continuous quality improvement.

References

Angelo, T. A., and Cross, K. P. *Classroom Assessment Techniques: A Handbook for College Teachers.* (2nd ed.) San Francisco: Jossey-Bass, 1993.

Atkinson, P. E. *Creating Culture Change: The Key to Successful Total Quality Management.* San Francisco: Pfeiffer, 1990.

Berry, E., Filbeck, M., Rothstein-Fisch, C., and Saltman, H. "Implementing Classroom Research in a State University: A Developmental Process." In T. A. Angelo (ed.), *Classroom Research: Early Lessons from Success.* New Directions for Teaching and Learning, no. 46. San Francisco: Jossey-Bass, 1991.

Bogue, E. G., and Saunders, R. L. *The Evidence for Quality: Strengthening the Tests of Academic and Administrative Effectiveness.* San Francisco: Jossey-Bass, 1992.

Cottell, P. G., Jr. "Classroom Research in Accounting: Assessing for Learning." In T. A. Angelo (ed.), *Classroom Research: Early Lessons from Success.* New Directions for Teaching and Learning, no. 46. San Francisco: Jossey-Bass, 1991.

Cross, K. P. "Classroom Research: Helping Professors Learn More About Teaching." In P. Seldin and Associates, *How Administrators Can Improve Teaching: Moving from Talk to Action in Higher Education.* San Francisco: Jossey-Bass, 1990.

Cross, K. P., and Angelo, T. A. "Faculty Members as Classroom Researchers." *Community, Technical and Junior College Journals,* 1989, *59* (5), 23–25.

Cuevas, G. J. "Feedback from Classroom Research Projects." *Community-Junior College Quarterly of Research and Practice,* 1991, *15* (4), 381–390.

Deming, W. E. *Out of the Crisis.* Cambridge, Mass.: MIT Press, 1986.

Kelly, D. "Classroom Research and Interactive Learning: Assessing the Impact on Adult Learners and Faculty." Doctoral dissertation, Claremont Graduate School, Claremont, Calif., 1993. *Dissertation Abstracts International.* (Order Number DA 9330348)

Kozma, R. B. "Communication, Rewards, and the Use of Classroom Innovations." *Journal of Higher Education,* 1979, *50* (6), 761–771.

Schauerman, S., and Peachy, B. *Strategies for Implementation: The El Camino TQM Story.* Torrance, Calif.: El Camino College, 1993. (ERIC Document Reproduction Service No. ED 355988)

Senge, P. *The Fifth Discipline: The Art and Practice of the Learning Organization.* New York: Doubleday, 1990.

Seymour, D. T. *Once Upon a Campus.* Phoenix, Ariz.: Oryx Press, 1995.

Steadman, M. H. *Implementation and Impact of Classroom Assessment Techniques in Community Colleges.* Unpublished doctoral dissertation, University of California, Berkeley, 1994. (UMI Microform no. 9528688)

Watkins, K. E., and Marsick, V. J. *Sculpting the Learning Organization: Lessons in the Art and Science of Systemic Change.* San Francisco: Jossey-Bass, 1993.

ELAINE SOETAERT is a consultant in Organizational Development Services at the Northern Alberta Institute of Technology.

PART THREE

New Applications, New
Considerations

Working together, three faculty members from different disciplines see the similarities and differences in their classes through the use of CATs.

Classroom Assessment Across the Disciplines

Regina Eisenbach, Vicki Golich, Renee Curry

> We may compare teaching to selling commodities. No one can sell unless someone buys . . . [yet] there are teachers who think they have done a good day's teaching irrespective of what pupils have learned.
>
> —Dewey, 1933, p. 35.

Funny, though the twenty-first century dawns, not much has changed for college and university faculty. We still confront the challenge of delivering comprehensive course content within arbitrarily limited time frames. Most of us graduate from programs that label research "the scholarship of discovery" (Boyer, 1990) and value it above all else. Then we move on to work in institutions of higher education that perpetuate this focus. Though few of these institutions would exist or survive without students, they seldom regard or reward the difficult and complex art and "scholarship of teaching" as highly as the scholarship of discovery. Consequently, many of us concentrate on transmitting vast amounts of information to our students using the conventional pedagogy of the lecture. Many remain convinced that "teaching is telling, knowledge is facts, and learning is recall" (Cohen, 1989).

As if these traditional obstacles to teaching were not enough, the approaching century adds some new, significant challenges to pedagogical success. First, the explosion of disciplinary information and theoretical thinking greatly complicates the selection of course materials. Second, institutions charge faculty with demonstrably improving inadequate learning outcomes (Ehrmann, 1995, p. 6) in the face of expanding diverse student populations *and* shrinking financial support. Employers seek skilled and knowledgeable graduates prepared to solve increasingly complex problems in various work environments. To deliver this "product," faculty must adopt pedagogies that empower students to identify the tools and information appropriate for the problem and enable students to assume roles as both effective leaders and team players (Ehrmann, 1995, p. 12).

Finally, research continues to demonstrate that the lecture—while an efficient mode for transferring information in the short term—is ineffective if we want students to remember that information over time. Students forget as much as 50 percent of course content within a few months of taking lecture-based courses (Stice, 1987). Current national trends that recognize the importance of excellent teaching have not been accompanied by professional development support. No wonder many of us feel overwhelmed.

Fortunately, Classroom Assessment Techniques (CATs) offer a relatively simple means to meet and overcome these significant challenges. By helping professors "obtain useful feedback on what, how much, and how well their students are learning," CATs enable faculty to refocus their teaching so students can make their learning more efficient and more effective" (Angelo and Cross, 1993, p. 3). In short, CATs help faculty concentrate on how, what, and at what pace students learn key concepts, assumptions, and analytical frameworks that inform every discipline.

Classroom Assessment and Effective Pedagogy

For years researchers have agreed on at least three principles of good practice in the teaching and learning process: active learning, frequent feedback on performance, and frequent student-faculty contact (see, for example, Dewey, 1933; Chickering and Gamson, 1987; Ewell and Jones, 1991). In addition, a substantial body of literature links pedagogies that support these principles to the enhancement of learning (see, for example, Association of American Colleges, 1985; McKeachie, Pintrich, Lin, and Smith, 1986; Pascarella and Terenzini, 1991). CATs—by design and by measured results—embody these principles: they require active student participation and create a viable, continuous feedback loop between faculty and students, thereby satisfying the need for frequent feedback and student-faculty contact. Together, these activities help students take responsibility for their learning and at the same time enhance the quality of student learning. CATs have the added benefit of adaptability: faculty can and should adapt them to the particular needs and characteristics of their students, their disciplines, and their own preferred teaching styles (Angelo and Cross, 1993, pp. 4–6).

Background to the Project

California State University at San Marcos (CSUSM) established a Faculty Center in the spring semester of 1995 in response to faculty demand for support of their multiple roles. Vicki Golich, associate professor of political science, was appointed as the first director of the center. Shortly thereafter she introduced CATs to Renee Curry, associate professor of literature and writing, and Regina Eisenbach, assistant professor of management. They were intrigued, and agreed to participate in a pilot to explore and document the value of CATs in a variety of disciplinary and course level settings—which we were well placed to do, as each of us taught a different student population: majors, general education students, and graduate students, respectively.

We selected CATs that we thought would be most adaptable to each of our content areas and course objectives. We decided early in the process to incorporate this new teaching strategy into those we already used successfully. We operated according to the belief that adopting new pedagogies only makes sense if value is added to the students' learning process. Each of us already used, and continues to use, instruments designed to measure student learning, such as quizzes, tests, papers, and oral examinations. By using CATs, we hoped to assess learning for development purposes rather than for grading purposes.

After choosing and adapting particular CATs—a mid-semester evaluation, pre and post confidence surveys, one minute papers, and muddiest point—we agreed on times during the semester to employ each but also allowed individual variations. We wanted to collect evidence that would be comparable, but we also wanted to test the flexibility and adaptability of the techniques. We met three times throughout the semester to discuss CAT results and to share ideas about the CAT procedure.

Description of CATs Used

The first CAT we adapted was the course-related self-confidence survey (Angelo and Cross, 1993); we called it the "pre/post" self-confidence survey. This technique measures student content knowledge at the beginning and end of a course. Each of us chose ten terms or ideas important in our individual courses. We asked students, "How confident do you feel that you could explain the following concepts to your friends or your parents?" Students completed the "Pre" survey and kept it until the end of the semester when we had them complete the "Post" survey. Both surveys had the same ten terms, allowing students to compare the two to see how much they had learned.

At mid-semester, we created our own teacher-designed feedback forms (Angelo and Cross, 1993) to evaluate student perceptions of our course reading materials and format. There were scaled items as well as two open-ended questions.

Throughout the semester, students answered variations on the minute paper (Angelo and Cross, 1993). One version asked students, "What information that we have covered today could have practical application for you outside the classroom?" The other was "What was the muddiest point in today's class session?" Students answered these questions briefly at the beginning or end of a class period.

Interpreting the Feedback

The three CATs yielded valuable information regarding student learning and general perceptions about our courses. To make the best use of this data, we needed to share the results with the class by either a summary or a discussion. This completed feedback loop showed students that we took their responses seriously; we spent valuable class time discussing them and frequently made changes to the course based on this input.

Mid-Semester Feedback Evaluation. For all three of us, the quantitative section of this questionnaire pointed out areas of strength and areas for improvement. What was additionally surprising was how similar our results were despite the differences in the contexts in which we taught. Most students in all three courses were satisfied with the reading materials, format, and knowledge the course provided. The open-ended comments led each of us to make important modifications at the midpoint of the semester based on the student input. In the sections that follow each of us will speak in turn from the first-person perspective.

Eisenbach's Management Class. In my management course, students believed that group activities, the class atmosphere, and focus on learning instead of memorizing were the best things about the class. The negative comments concerned the exam format—"too much material, too little time"—and the amount of outside time spent on the group project. In the large group discussion, I explained how the interrelationship among the chapters required that they be assigned together. And I designed the exam questions to integrate the knowledge in these related areas. Regarding the group project, the information from this CAT provided me the opportunity to reiterate the importance of working with groups outside of regular class time.

Golich's Political Science Class. In my political science course, the open-ended comments revealed that the students appreciated the real-world examples found in the case studies used. Typically, negative comments focused on the amount of reading required and the "dry" nature of the textbook; others expressed concerns about the emphasis on political economy since most political science courses are less interdisciplinary in approach. Perhaps the most critical outcomes of this evaluation derived from two different student comments that led to important "teachable moments." First, a student wrote that she did not like "how I feel 'duh' after we discuss a case study." When I reported the results of the overall evaluation, I commented that I wished I knew more concretely what that comment meant, since my goal was to help folks feel smarter, not dumber! This brave student identified herself and explained that she thought she should be able to solve the complex issues in the cases alone; that her individual knowledge should be comprehensive enough to do this on her own. I was able to explain that one person rarely solves the real problems "out there"; rather, teamwork is imperative for identifying and implementing solutions. This had a tremendous empowering effect for the students, who had been trained to believe they should be able to do it all on their own.

The second instance came from a student who commented that I should change "everything," and that there was literally "nothing" to like about the course. During the feedback discussion, it became clear that this student was an outlier. I was able to explain that I could not and would not change "everything," and that, what is more important, if a class really needs an overhaul, comments must be more specific to help a professor implement the desired changes. These opportunities to clarify course goals and activities appear to engage students powerfully in their learning processes.

Curry's Literature and Writing Class. Finally, in my literature and writing course, the open-ended comments demonstrated that the students liked the class discussions and the variety of approaches to teaching. Most students perceived the course as useful and effective in attaining the goals of the course, which include reading, analyzing, and theorizing about the texts written by Toni Morrison as well as those written about her work.

Interestingly, 47 percent of the students suggested that we spend more time on the texts written by Morrison and less on the secondary texts. This response afforded me a wonderful opportunity to discuss with these first-semester master's students what it meant to be graduate students in literature and writing. The students and I discussed the importance of literary criticism and theory to the work of scholars and creative writers. Without this CAT, I would have assumed that graduate students inherently knew that the treatment of secondary texts increased as they moved into the master's world.

Pre/Post Self-Confidence Survey. The pre/post survey results demonstrated a dramatic shift in student confidence. The pre surveys show the vast majority of students not feeling confident about their knowledge of the ten concepts. The post surveys show the exact opposite; students in all three courses reported a much higher level of confidence at the end of the semester.

Eisenbach's Management Class. In my management class, the results of the post survey impressed the students. Comments such as "this proves we learned something" were common. There was, however, one term that students did not understand. I was initially concerned. The term, "Hofstede Framework," should have been familiar to the students since it was recently covered in class. In the feedback session, I asked about the framework without referring to its "formal name" and the students were able to answer correctly. Had they not understood the underlying framework, students would not have been able to answer the questions. Thus, this CAT helped me clarify the importance of knowing the appropriate terminology that corresponds to theoretical models.

Golich's Political Science Class. Likewise, in my political science class, students were extremely happy with the results of the pre/post self-confidence surveys. Typical comments included the following: "I really like the pre and post test. Although the pre test was embarrassing, I was happy to fill out the post." "This CAT makes you more aware of these terms as you come across them in your readings." And, "I liked the pre and post surveys because it gave the course structure and showed what I learned over the semester." In the one instance where students did not feel significantly more confident, I knew why!

I included the term "Postmodernism" in the surveys even though I knew we would not cover it very explicitly in the course. When students registered fewer "very confident" results for this term, I explained the importance of both class time and external reading to the learning process. That students felt less confident about this term indicated that we had not dealt with this concept effectively in class.

Curry's Literature and Writing Class. Again in my literature and writing course, the students enjoyed reviewing their post self-confidence surveys. Similar to an occurrence in political science, one student reported a "decrease" in self-confidence regarding the "Black woman writer" concept. This student wrote on the form "Now I do not think I know 'wimmin' at all." Upon discussing this issue in class, we determined that phrases or labels initially appearing self-explanatory can become more complex, more political, and more controversial after further analysis. Therefore, self-confidence with a concept may decrease, indicating a more humble position toward the material rather than a failure to understand it.

Minute Paper and Muddiest Point. We all used the minute paper and muddiest point CAT at least twice during the semester. This CAT proved most beneficial in helping us to modify our style and pace of delivery. It provided particularly powerful "teachable moments" by allowing us to witness the exact intellectual struggle that was occurring for the students, and then to provoke students in their thinking processes. The combination of anonymity and faculty interest in student learning outcomes inspired honest, articulate responses from the students.

In the end, students commented that the minute paper proved incredibly valuable to their individual and collective learning processes. In a separate evaluation at the end of the semester in the political science course, they offered the following sample comments: "The minute paper allowed the class to participate in the lecture and allowed you to clarify tough questions." "It really helped to clarify the reading." "It helped you [Dr. Golich] to see what we still did not understand." "I felt as though I learned the material, rather than simply being familiar with it." "When you feel you have a 'dumb' question, this helps." "This one tests to see if students are ready for class, encourages students to become better prepared." Perhaps most important, "The anticipation of doing this helped me keep up with the readings."

Sharing the Results. In addition to sharing the information with students, we met once a month to show each other the results of each CAT. This meeting provided us the opportunity to process the information at a deeper level. The questions and comments we made to each other led us to reexamine the rationale behind our teaching methods. For the first time, we made explicit the assumptions underlying the way we teach our courses. Moreover, our discussions led us to test the validity of these assumptions. Thus our sharing sessions became opportunities for personal growth and development.

An added benefit of our regular meetings was the emotional support we received from each other. Sharing negative information about our teaching placed each of us in a vulnerable position. However, the positive atmosphere of our group turned feelings of anxiety into feelings of confidence.

For example, one of us used the muddiest point to check whether students had done the reading. Unfortunately, most students had not prepared for that day's class. Using e-mail to explain this upsetting result allowed the rest of us to recommend courses of action and offer our understanding. This support helped defuse the potential anger and instead allowed an in-class discussion of what it means to be prepared for class. Again, this reinforced the students' responsibility for their own learning. They came to realize that not doing the reading meant they missed out on important information. Thus the instant feedback from colleagues allowed a "teachable moment" to occur in that class.

Conclusion

CATs provide professors with significant information about the value of course content and the sometimes mysterious process of student learning. Creating and using CATs reminded us that the most effective teaching begins with clear goals for the entire course and for each individual class session. CATs contribute to self-reflection by both professors and students. Designing CATs helps faculty stay focused on course and class goals; responding to CATs requires students to concentrate on course material and to think about what they are learning. Thus, CATs demand a reciprocal effort from teacher and student to stay involved in the learning process throughout the semester.

It takes courage and self-confidence to work with CATs because we must face and respond to occasional negative response from students. Therefore, faculty have to feel ready to use CATs. Readiness often suggests we feel the need to take a reality check on what is or is not working in our classes. It implies that we consider change may be necessary and desirable. At the same time, CATs provide opportunities for students to articulate why they may not want to make certain changes. By forcing us to return to our learning goals repeatedly, CATs encourage a self-reflection which can let us know what change needs consideration, when such a change warrants consideration, and why articulation of learning objectives needs repetition.

This chapter describes a cross-sectional study that compares CAT values across two dimensions, disciplines and course levels. We have described how the use of CATs fosters improved communication and reflection. We invite readers to try this themselves; the experience will be both refreshing and rewarding.

References

Angelo, T. A., and Cross, K. P. *Classroom Assessment Techniques: A Handbook for College Teachers.* (2nd ed.) San Francisco: Jossey-Bass, 1993.

Association of American Colleges. *Integrity in the College Curriculum: A Report to the Academic Community.* Washington, D.C.: Association of American Colleges, 1985.

Boyer, E. L. *Scholarship Reconsidered: Priorities of the Professoriate.* Princeton, N.J.: Carnegie

Foundation for the Advancement of Teaching, 1990.

Chickering, A. W., and Gamson, Z. F. "Seven Principles for Good Practice in Undergraduate Education." *AAHE Bulletin,* 1987, *39,* 3–7.

Cohen, D. K. "Teaching Practice: *Plus ça Change. . . .*" In P. W. Jackson (ed.), *Contributing to Educational Change: Perspectives on Research and Practice.* Berkeley, Calif.: McCutchan, 1989.

Dewey, J. *How We Think.* Lexington, Mass.: Heath, 1933.

Ehrmann, S. C. "Local Assessment of Educational Strategies That Use Computing, Video, and Telecommunications." Commissioned paper prepared for AAHE's 10th Annual Conference on Assessment and Quality, Boston, Mass., June 11–14, 1995.

Ewell, P. T., and Jones, D. P. "Actions Matter: The Case for Indirect Measures in Assessing Higher Education's Progress on the National Education Goals." *Journal of General Education,* 1991, 42 (2), 123–148.

McKeachie, W. J., Pintrich, P. R., Lin, Y. G., and Smith, D. *Teaching and Learning in the College Classroom: A Review of the Research Literature.* Ann Arbor, Mich.: National Center for Research to Improve Postsecondary Teaching and Learning (NCRIPTAL), University of Michigan, 1986.

Pascarella, F. T., and Terenzini, P. T. *How College Affects Students: Findings and Insight From Twenty Years of Research.* San Francisco: Jossey-Bass, 1991.

Stice, J. E. "Using Kolb's Learning Cycle to Improve Student Learning." *Engineering Education,* 1987, 77, 291–296.

REGINA EISENBACH *is associate professor and center director, Center for Service Sector Management in the College of Business at California State University at San Marcos.*

VICKI L. GOLICH *is professor of political science and director of the Faculty Center at California State University at San Marcos.*

RENEE CURRY *is associate professor of literature and writing at California State University at San Marcos.*

Implementing Classroom Assessment and Research beyond the confines of a single institution poses special problems, but offers special rewards as well.

A Minnesota Story: A System Approach to Classroom Assessment and Research

Joel Peterson, Connie Stack

This is the story of a statewide system of colleges that decided to make Classroom Assessment and Research a major theme for faculty development. While our situation as a system may be unique, we believe the elements of our success and difficulties are transferable to any learning organization.

Although the system of colleges in question is now called Minnesota State Colleges and Universities (MnSCU), our story has its roots in the culture of the Minnesota Community College System—one of the three systems that merged to form MnSCU in 1995. Part of our present faculty development mission is to spread the word about Classroom Assessment and Research to our new colleagues in Minnesota's seven state universities and thirty-four technical colleges, while continuing to nurture its maturing development on our twenty-one community college campuses.

The terms *Classroom Assessment* and *Classroom Research* first entered our community college faculty development vocabulary in the fall of 1989. Seven years later, these terms have become household words among the approximately five hundred faculty (out of sixteen hundred) who regularly participate in faculty development. The multiple yellow and blue copies of Angelo and Cross's *Classroom Assessment Techniques: A Handbook for College Teachers* (1993) have become dog-eared and stained. Much like a well-used family cookbook, *Classroom Assessment Techniques* keeps providing faculty who search through

Note: We owe special recognition to Walter Cullen, our retired director of faculty development, who has shaped the sustained, supported, integrated program described in this chapter. Jane Harmon, now president of Adirondack Community College in Queensbury, New York, deserves the credit for initiating our Classroom Assessment and Research program and running it during its first two years as part of her doctoral program.

it with new ideas and applications that will change the way they do things tomorrow.

The key words in the successful part of our story are *sustained, supported, integrated,* and *showcased.* The key words in the problematic part are *research, grading,* and *gimmick.*

Coping with Negative Impact

Let's start with the problematic part.

Research. The most common cause of mischief we have encountered in trying to interest faculty in Classroom Assessment and Research is the word *research.* For many of us in academia, we cannot hear that word without the notions of hard data, baselines, and experimental versus control groups coming immediately to mind. The very next thought is usually "There's no way I have the time or energy to do research on what happens in my classroom on top of *teaching* the class."

Now, to be sure, there is nothing wrong with doing this kind of ambitious educational research. But it is paradoxically both more and less than what we are hoping to get faculty to do. It is obviously more work—more of an additional burden on top of teaching—than we had in mind. But at the same time it is less than what we want to see. What we see as the power of Classroom Assessment is that it is *formative* rather than *summative* assessment.

It's the presupposition that counts here. Formative assessment is done midcourse to see whether there may be some corrections that will help bring us more happily to our destination. Formative assessment presupposes the willingness to change—perhaps even the desire to improve. Summative assessment can be used this way too—in the longer perspective of changing courses over the years. But summative assessment most often serves other goals. Formative assessment aims at making changes tomorrow that will help the learners I am working with today. Formative assessment engages these learners in a process designed primarily to enhance their learning, and only secondarily to improve my teaching.

Another power we see in Classroom Assessment is more radical. It is tied up in the notion that if you use the practice, you owe it to your students to give them collective feedback on the assessment—not grades. This is often the scariest part for teachers. It's hard enough if you discover, midcourse, students are having some kind of problem in your class. But having to report back to your students that significant numbers of them think there is a problem in your class can be very threatening. It pushes you to do one or more of three things: make some change in how you are managing the class, explain why you believe it's important *not* to change the way you are managing the class, or ask for their suggestions on how to solve the problem. Whichever way you go, something very central in the dynamic of the traditional classroom has begun to change: the inalienable right of teachers to rule their classroom.

It takes significant courage for most teachers to take that first step toward reporting the results of Classroom Assessment back to the class.

Acknowledging that, however, we have yet to hear a teacher who has taken that first step say anything bad came of it. What we hear, usually along with the surprise of the teacher, is how appreciative the students were and how they began to take more interest in the way the class was run and more responsibility for their own role in it. Quite often, especially where the teacher has invited discussion of the problem, we hear that Classroom Assessment has initiated a change in the dynamics of the classroom toward a more collaborative community of learners.

Grading. The second problematic aspect of introducing the notion of Classroom Assessment and Research to faculty is the automatic assumption that assessment and grades are inextricably linked. This assumption manifests itself in either surprise or blank stares when you say that Classroom Assessment Techniques are ungraded and anonymous. Why would anyone want to take the time and effort to identify an appropriate Classroom Assessment Technique and to administer and evaluate it if it's not going to be counted as part of the students' grades? And how could we ever hope to get students to take these assessments seriously if they "don't count for anything?"

Here again, the first step takes a leap of faith. In our experience, we have never heard a teacher who has used Classroom Assessment Techniques ungraded and anonymously report any problem in students' motivation or their perception of the value of the activity. Of course, knowing their comments are anonymous and cannot affect their grade makes a huge difference in students' perception of the risk involved in telling you honestly what's working and what's not, as well as what they understand and what they don't.

There is another reason why we often find teachers are using Classroom Assessment Techniques as graded assignments. The truth is, many of the CATs described in *Classroom Assessment Techniques*—especially those focused on subject content rather than students' perception of their learning—make excellent graded assignments. There is absolutely nothing wrong with this. In fact, we encourage faculty to use *Classroom Assessment Techniques* as a resource for tasks for performance assessment. But we ask them not to confuse this use of the strategies to assess *student performance* with the very different use of the same tasks to provide formative, anonymous assessment of the *teacher's performance* in managing the classroom learning experience.

Why is this distinction important? We can think of two reasons—one from the students' perspective and one from the teacher's. From the students' side, if it is their performance that is being evaluated and it counts for their grade, then the simplest risk-analysis makes it clear that they are better off bluffing or trying to guess what the teacher wants to hear than being honest. This contaminates the value of the results for any purpose of formative evaluation.

From the teacher's point of view, on the other hand, grading always requires careful attention to standards and fairness in assigning marks that are publicly defensible. The care, time, and effort this takes will act as a strong deterrent to frequent use of Classroom Assessment Techniques. It is much easier—and truer to the spirit of CATs—to quickly read through the results (or even to do a random sampling) and look for patterns that give you an overall picture of how the class as a whole is going and what changes might make it go better.

Gimmick. One last problematic aspect of Classroom Assessment and Research is teachers' great love of gimmicks—something new and relatively easy to plug into class the Monday following the Friday conference. On one level, there is nothing wrong with being constantly on the lookout for a new teaching strategy to add to our teaching toolbox. New approaches to learning add variety and texture to our classrooms. Carried to the extreme, however, this search for something new can have two deleterious effects. The first is that the strategy—for example, the muddiest point CAT—is inserted in Monday's class without much thought to the details, goals, or implications of bringing Classroom Assessment into your teaching, or into this specific class. Some of the things we have seen happen include not giving feedback to students on the results, becoming discouraged or even angry over the things students say they don't understand, succumbing to frustration and stress at realizing you have to go back over old material while the class gets further and further behind where the syllabus says the class should be, and consequently feeling strong disinclination to introduce further Classroom Assessment Techniques.

The second problem is that gimmicks have a tendency to be overused so that they go from novel to routine to burdensome. In one of our projects we asked students to keep journals of their daily experiences over the course of a quarter. One of the most common problems students reported was the use of a once-innovative teaching strategy again and again and again in a way that appeared to students to be a rather mindless substitute for some more traditional mode of teaching.

The most successful uses of Classroom Assessment Techniques we have seen start from careful consideration of the nature and value of Classroom Assessment and its implications for classroom dynamics. This is then followed by a search to identify a particular CAT from *Classroom Assessment Techniques* that best suits a particular purpose in a specific lesson. CATs in these classrooms are varied and paced to fit the flow of the course and nature of the material being studied. They are a means to further ends, and not a gimmick to try as an end in itself.

Positive Results

That brings us through the dark side of our experience with Classroom Assessment and Research to the brighter side of our story, and what we believe are the most important factors contributing to our measure of success.

Sustained. The structure of faculty development as it has evolved in Minnesota's system of community colleges is rooted in three factors: a history of focused, six-year foundation grants; a faculty union leadership committed to bargaining for an institutionalized, systemwide approach to improving teaching and learning; and a system office congenial to expanding programs to help its twenty-one campuses do their work better. As a result, our efforts in faculty development have always taken the long-term approach. We have had no one-shot conferences on a hot topic, nor have we had an ever-changing progression of one-year teaching initiatives.

We have had two six-year external grants, one in writing across the curriculum, one in critical thinking. Our program in Classroom Assessment and Research has been modeled on these two external grants—but the funding has been entirely from within the system. Each program has been sustained, albeit in a somewhat reduced form, after the original funding ran out. Writing across the curriculum, for example, was in its eleventh year at the date of this writing.

The principle behind this long-term approach is our belief that, given a teaching strategy as rich as Classroom Assessment and Research, you risk doing more damage than good by thinking of faculty development cycles in any less than three-year spans, and that the program and its benefits only really begin to take off in the fifth year.

Every movement has its early joiners. We had nearly eighty faculty who were interested enough in Classroom Assessment after our first fall conference come back for a follow-up conference in the spring. But even the leaders among this group were disheartened to realize, the following fall in conference with an outside consultant, that for the most part, they still didn't get it. It wasn't until the third year that a significant core of faculty began to finally understand the broader picture and to see the kinds of changes in teaching and classroom dynamics that go along with a serious commitment to Classroom Assessment and Research. Only then did we start getting significant numbers of well-thought-out reports about the integral use of CATs leading to mid-course improvements and to discovery of intriguing patterns in learners' perceptions of their learning experience. Each year since that third year the number of faculty who "get it" has improved dramatically.

Our learning curve undoubtedly would have been faster if the big blue and yellow *Classroom Assessment Techniques* had been published before our fourth year. But we have a hard time imagining a situation where it would take any less than two years before you begin to reach the point of critical mass beyond which Classroom Assessment and Research begins to take off and grow exponentially. Thinking in shorter time span seems to us an invitation to dabbling and the "tried it, done it, been there" end result.

Supported. In our experience, conferences and workshops are an absolutely necessary condition for effective pedagogical change, but they are far from being a sufficient condition.

Higher Community. The need to come together to learn of innovations in teaching has both skill and motivational components. Conferences allow faculty the opportunity to come into contact with the experts. There is more to this than the obvious fact that the experts have honed their expertise in training faculty. Experts also bring with them an enthusiasm and excitement—a sense of missionary zeal—which these voices from the outside generally can impart far more effectively than anyone from within the community could.

There are two aspects to this. We all know it is not necessarily the case that the experts really are better trainers, technically, than our own faculty leaders are. But we also all know the common saying that no one from our own campus can possibly be an expert. We give to experts an aura of awe and respect that we cannot possibly give our colleague in the office next to us, whose strengths and inadequacies as a teacher and presenter are necessarily comparable to our own. So it is valuable to bring in outsiders because, in general, outside experts generate the respect that draws faculty in and gets things started on a high plane of expectations. Second, outside experts are in a better position to exhort us to "join the movement" and send us back to our campuses charged up for thinking globally and acting locally. When our colleague in the next office talks this way, chances are we'll think of Don Quixote off tilting at windmills again.

There is one other aspect of conferences that has been very important in our experience. Because our conferences are systemwide—not campuswide—they create for each of us a sense of being part of a larger community of dedicated, concerned teachers. This is a very important feeling that we suspect may not be achievable on the campus level. We are tempted to argue that sustained pedagogical change may not be spiritually feasible if it is not supported by some sense of belonging to a community of like-minded souls beyond the pettiness and power struggles of our immediate campus community. We have found that faculty who do not think of themselves as leaders locally *are* empowered to think of themselves as educational leaders when they find their work is valued by communities beyond their immediate campus. Our community of systemwide faculty development partisans provides this higher community. There is something decidedly spiritual about ritual gatherings of faculty at seasonal conferences that puts them back in touch with a higher community, sends them forth to do good work, and reminds them they have higher resources to turn to if things get tough.

However, the support from above provided by conferences is not enough. In our experience, local support is equally essential.

Campus Community. Local support is qualitatively different from what conferences can offer. Local support is rooted in the ups and downs, the crises and the successes, the skills and the encouragement of day-to-day teaching.

We are fortunate to have system funding that provides stipends or release time for faculty leaders on each campus to coordinate each of our major faculty development initiatives. These leaders are charged with being both the encouragers and the technical support staff for local faculty development. They give faculty who are trying new things in the classroom the assurance there is personal and professional help close at hand. Part of the leaders' job is to provide individualized support for faculty—help in finding just the right CAT for a specific teaching question, or help in figuring out what sense to make of the results.

In addition, the leaders form a collaborative team charged with planning, publicizing, and hosting a program of regular faculty development sessions on their own campus. Sometimes these sessions involve presentations by local colleagues, colleagues from other campuses, or external experts. Other meetings are devoted to sharing success stories or concentrating the group's experience and creative problem-solving abilities on the teaching problems someone brings to the group. Often there is food. Always there should be camaraderie.

One essential ingredient for making this support system work is that colleagues must feel safe in voluntarily sharing their syllabi and assignments, their problems and their students' negative comments—as well as their successes and positive feedback. This has become a part of our culture. Faculty and administrators feel a deep respect for the work done by their colleagues and for the effort they put into trying to become better teachers. The administrators who have taken an interest in faculty development are, by and large, trusted and respected by faculty and their participation as equals is welcomed as a good sign of support. Although we have done all we can to build a structure for systemwide and local support for faculty who are willing to try something new, in the final analysis the most important element for supporting innovation is the culture of our system and the local campus.

Here is a story to illustrate this point. In the days before we had a good system of local support for new techniques, we had an outstanding systemwide conference on collaborative learning. At a meeting two years later as part of a site visit for a new grant, a teacher told the following story. "I remember going to a conference . . . I think it was on collaborative learning. I came back from the conference all excited about trying it out the next week. I did. It didn't go over real well. I did try it one other time, but then the pressure was on, I had piles of papers to grade and I was worried about getting behind on my syllabus. I never tried it again." That prompted another teacher to say:

> I was at the same conference. Learning about collaborative learning at that conference has done more to improve my teaching than anything else before or since. But what happened in our case is that three of us who went to that conference together decided afterward we would get together every week and talk about how our attempts at implementing collaborative learning techniques were going. We all felt that same initial feeling that it didn't work very well, that it meant more work for us (at least at the start) and that we would have trouble keeping up with our syllabi. But it became a matter of honor and responsibility for each other that we keep on getting together each week and that we had tried some new technique or modified an old one so that we had something to report to the others. It was this bond to colleagues that kept us going when things got tough which motivated us to see it through and to come to see how powerful an approach to learning it is.

If you really want to help faculty make a change as potentially powerful as that prompted by Classroom Assessment and Research, the challenge is how can you create this kind of bond of shared support, responsibility, and respect among like-minded colleagues who have heard the call. Don't send faculty to conferences alone. Keep bringing them together afterward.

Integrated. We started our work in Classroom Assessment and Research six years ago with a fall and a spring conference. Effort was made to get everyone who attended the fall conference to commit to "assessing something" in one of their classes, and to bring the results back to the spring conference. Despite heroic effort by the system coordinator, there was considerable confusion. Very few projects were consummated. In the following two years we gained considerable ground on understanding, but to some extent the confusion persisted. In part, we think the problem was related to the abstractness of the injunction to "assess something."

What we have come to realize is that it is much easier to come to an understanding of Classroom Assessment and Research if it is integrated with other teaching concerns—like critical thinking, writing across the curriculum, active learning, or more generally, improving learning. The problem is one of means and ends.

Classroom Assessment and Research is not an end in itself. It is a means to some other pedagogical end. Put another way, the fifty CATs in *Classroom Assessment Techniques* are fifty different tools that teachers can use for a variety of different purposes in the classroom. The reflective practitioner uses them for one or more of three basic purposes: to find out something about what students know, to find out something about how students are learning, or to help students develop specific skills of self-conscious learning.

When we came to understand that Classroom Assessment and Research was not an end in itself, we made a conscious decision to make it an essential part of *everything* we do in faculty development. In all our presentations we model the use of Classroom Assessment Techniques. Whenever faculty give presentations on innovative teaching strategies at our conferences, we urge them both to include results of Classroom Research on their innovations and also to use at least one CAT in their presentation. In all projects faculty undertake for stipends or for graduate credit, we require that they be assessed using at least one CAT from *Classroom Assessment Techniques*.

We no longer ask faculty to "assess something." We ask them to create and pilot-test a new critical thinking or writing across the curriculum strategy in their courses, to use CATs to formatively assess the results, and to share those results with colleagues. We also demonstrate how to use CATs as an instructional strategy to develop skills in both our critical thinking and writing across the curriculum initiatives. The result is a lot less confusion and a lot more interest.

Showcased. When the work done by faculty in a faculty development program like Classroom Assessment and Research is showcased, it is a little like an orchard in springtime. The orchard may have appeared dormant, but suddenly the work of several teachers begins to blossom. Others follow, as if encouraged by those first blossoms. And soon there is a lot of buzzing and a lot of cross-pollination of ideas. Afterward, the orchard gets on with the less showy but essential work of growth and ripening that culminates in the harvest of mature fruit.

We showcase faculty work in three major ways: workshops, publications, and word of mouth.

First, all our systemwide conferences—and a lot of our campus work group meetings—prominently feature workshop presentations led by our faculty on strategies they have developed, piloted, and assessed. We have also begun to use GIFT sessions—Great Ideas for Teaching—in which presenters sit at tables and give a series of ten or so six-minute presentations. Every ten minutes a bell rings and everyone gets up and chooses another table presentation.

We strongly encourage our presenters to *show* rather than to *tell* so that the sessions demonstrate good active learning principles. We also require that the presentation include a Classroom Assessment Technique and results. In over eight years of showcasing faculty work at conferences, we have noted that quite consistently, the workshops led by our faculty are given extremely high evaluation marks—as high as those given by our best nationally recognized presenters, or higher. Our faculty are proud of the work of their colleagues, and at the same time, they are encouraged by the fact that teachers just like them, teaching in the same conditions, can do such outstanding work. This often serves as an antidote to the feeling that the impressive teaching techniques advocated by an outside speaker don't translate very well to the context of a two-year college where faculty teach forty-five quarter credits with large classes and no graduate assistants. But what your colleagues can do, *you* could do—and you can ask them about all the details, and you can share with them the results.

A second way in which we showcase exemplary work by our faculty is to publish their work in an annual systemwide publication called *Open to Change,* written in a format derived from the reports in *Classroom Assessment Techniques.* Each year we choose approximately seventeen reports from a field of fifty to eighty submissions. We have funds to provide small honoraria for everyone who submits a report. This honorarium, in turn, enables us to require that each author work with his or her campus leader and work group over the course of the year in developing the teaching innovation, designing and analyzing the results, and writing the report.

A third means of showcasing faculty work is by word of mouth. We are constantly sharing with others within and outside our system the outstanding work our faculty are doing. Within the system, we are able to put teachers working on a new idea in touch with teachers we know who have done related work. In and out of our system, in our presentations we highlight and credit specific teaching innovations developed by our faculty. Contingent on travel funding, we invite faculty colleagues to present with us at national conferences as well as to submit proposals on their own.

Showcasing faculty work is both rewarding and essential for the growth of a faculty development initiative like Classroom Assessment and Research.

But you should be warned that—as in most things in life—timing is everything. We have said a few pages back that outside experts are better able to attract, train, and inspire faculty than can someone who has an office down the hall and who teaches in the room next to yours. This is true, we believe, at the beginning. But it is not eternally true. There comes a critical point at which a faculty development initiative has enough momentum and enough proponents doing excellent work that local talent becomes more effective than outside talent. How will you know when you've reached that point?

For that *you* need to do some Classroom Assessment. We had word-of-mouth reports from our campus leaders on each campus, but much of the time their knowledge of what individual faculty were doing was spotty. Phoning, interviewing, or observing faculty colleagues whom you have some reason to suspect are doing exemplary work would be extremely time-consuming. For us, the reports we encourage all our faculty development participants to submit have served as a form of Classroom Assessment that tells us how well our faculty have mastered the notion of Classroom Assessment itself. For the first two years we found the results rather discouraging. Roughly two-thirds of the reports that came in revealed major misconceptions about Classroom Research: many confounded it with teacher's impressions, course-end teacher evaluations, educational research, or grading. By the third year the numbers turned around and less than a quarter of the reports were flawed by misunderstandings of Classroom Research. At this point we began, in our conferences, to rely heavily on showcasing faculty work in concurrent and GIFT sessions and relying on outside presenters mainly to give opening and closing keynotes.

Lessons Learned

Our situation is unusual in that we came to Classroom Assessment and Research as a system of twenty-one community colleges with a coordinated, systemwide faculty development program. But even if you are in a situation where faculty development has always been handled completely locally, you can take some lessons from our experience.

If faculty development on your campus consists primarily of giving individuals money to attend conferences, try to get a group of faculty to go together to a Classroom Assessment and Research conference. Then make arrangements for the group to meet together regularly afterward to share successes and difficulties, support and advice. See if you can help each other write up reports on specific classroom applications of CATs and try to get them printed in campus publications, and perhaps in regional or national publications. Submit presentation proposals at regional and national conferences. Plan as a group to present your work in Classroom Assessment and Research in workshops or "brown-baggers" at your own campus. Seek out faculty development programs at other colleges that are emphasizing Classroom Assessment and Research and see if you can find profitable ways to join forces.

If faculty development on your campus is more programmatic, we urge you to make your work in Classroom Assessment and Research a sustained long-term program. On one level, Classroom Assessment and Research looks deceptively simple—like a bag of teaching tricks to try out to see which ones you like. On another level, however, they are powerful tools for changing the way most faculty do business by making the classroom more learner-centered and consonant with current research about how people learn best. You sell your faculty development program short if you settle for a one-shot presentation by an outside consultant. We think you sell your program short even if you make it a theme for a whole year. Make it a continuing theme, woven into all the other faculty development initiatives you do.

If you are in a system like ours, with a systemwide faculty development program, don't neglect the need for local support groups to help individuals keep the spirit alive and give them a circle of colleagues to turn to for sharing ideas and feedback. Use your conferences not just for bringing in an expert to present new Classroom Assessment and Research Techniques. Use them to help build and sustain a sense of camaraderie, community, and common goals. Find ways to identify exemplary work done by faculty and showcase their work increasingly at conferences and in publications.

Whatever level you are at and whatever system for using Classroom Assessment and Research you choose, the effort will be worthwhile in terms of the changes these techniques can bring about in faculty and on campuses.

Reference

Angelo, T. A., and Cross, K. P. *Classroom Assessment Techniques: A Handbook for College Teachers.* (2nd ed.) San Francisco: Jossey-Bass, 1993.

JOEL PETERSON *is dean of liberal arts and social sciences at Lake Superior College.*

CONNIE STACK *is coordinator for the Minnesota State Colleges and Universities Center for Teaching and Learning.*

Classroom Assessment Techniques are especially helpful to beginning teachers.

Using CATs to Help New Instructors Develop as Teachers

Laurie Richlin

One of the most pressing issues in the development of beginning instructors, particularly teaching assistants (TAs), is how to shift their teaching focus from survival issues to an interest in student learning. Sprague and Nyquist (1989) suggest three phases in the development of TAs: *senior learners, colleagues in training,* and *junior colleagues.* Graduate students are selected to be TAs because they are "expert students." These beginning TAs lack expert knowledge of the subject matter, the learning process, and the university system. In the senior learner stage, they begin to separate from their former role of student and begin to adopt the new one of teacher. TAs become colleagues in training during the transition stage. At this point in their development, TAs "become more concerned about their lack of teaching skills. . . . They begin to adapt teaching methods to their own personal styles and to figure out unique solutions to novel problems" (Sprague and Nyquist, 1989, p. 44). In the junior colleague stage, TAs begin to see themselves as colleagues with existing faculty in terms of both research and teaching.

Ronkowski (1993) identified nine TA concerns, which she divided into three stages based on Fuller's concerns model (Fuller and Brown, 1975): basic survival, skill improvement, and student learning. She found that the majority of TA concerns, regardless of amount of teaching experience, were at the survival level: adequacy of self as instructor and leader.

Svinicki, Sullivan, Greer, and Diaz created the prototype developmental scheme for TAs shown in Table 8.1, based on instructors' responses to areas of teaching concern. It shows the TAs' level of commitment to teaching and perceptions of self at different stages. Svinicki and the others identified a pre-stage, during which the new teachers are dualistic, either denying that they are real teachers or working hard to be "perfect." At stage 1, teachers are overpreparers, focused on content and suffering from "performance anxiety." By stage 2, they are looking outward at their students, whom they attempt to direct through manipulation. Finally, at stage 3, they see themselves as partners with their students in the learning enterprise.

Understanding the stages of instructor development provides guidance for planning training programs, assigning courses, supervising TA work, and

Table 8.1. Prototype of Responses to Some Areas of Teaching Concern at Different Developmental Levels

	Prestage	*Stage 1*	*Stage 2*	*Stage 3*
Areas of concern	I'm not really a teacher. OR, I will be a perfect teacher.	Can I do it right? Am I good enough to pull it off?	I'm orchestrating student learning.	Teaching is a partnership with the students, both individually and as a group.
Content and course planning	Imposed from outside.	Content is primary, most important thing.	Student grasp of content, motivation of students.	Content is secondary, meta concerns: seeing beyond the requirements, taking a more critical eye toward evaluative content.
Students	Idealized or unknown.	Irrelevant, the opposition.	Performing animals, reflection of instructor.	Partners, of primary importance.
Evaluation and monitoring progress	Don't think about it.	Clueless.	I have to fix it. Why do students rate my teaching this way?	Selectivity, discrimination, ability to perceive what does or doesn't come from oneself.
Methods	Alternatives exist?	Basic competency, learn to do with focus on me.	Reevaluate teaching, cause certain effects on students, learning to do it.	Choosing among methods, expertise.
Communication and presentation skills	Do I know enough to say?	Getting answer right. Can I do it? Performance anxiety.	Will students understand? Judging my communication by its effects on students.	Remove self from center of communication, communication or message becomes central.

Note: Additional areas of teaching concern described by Svinicki and others are sense of self in relationship to students, authority and discipline, and career concerns. See Richlin, 1995.

Source: Svinicki, Sullivan, Greer, and Diaz, 1991. Used with permission.

providing career mentoring. Designing activities to help new instructors move through the stages in each area of concern is an important strategy for assuring that graduate instructors are capable of doing the work they are assigned, and that new faculty will be ready to assume their teaching duties when they are hired.

Trying Various Strategies

During the dozen years I have worked with graduate instructors and new faculty, I have tried many different strategies to facilitate their movement from self-concern to interest in their students' learning. The major barrier has seemed to be the instructors' reluctance to break through the invisible wall separating their podium-prestige from the messiness of student needs. Perhaps some of the problem stems from the nature of graduate study and the hierarchical structure of academic life. Whatever the cause, new instructors have been wary of exposing themselves to the evaluation of their students. Their fear is exacerbated by the usual type of student feedback, which is collected near the end of the course (at a very sensitive time, often just prior to finals week) and not provided to the instructors until long after they can make any adjustments in the course. One of the laments I have heard most about end-of-term evaluations is "If only I'd known [whatever], I could have fixed it."

One technique that has helped to decrease instructor-student distance has been the Small Group Instructional Diagnosis (SGID), in which another instructor (or faculty development specialist) meets privately with the students during the last twenty minutes or so of a class period to ask questions such as: *What is the instructor doing right? What should the instructor do that is not being done now? What changes in instruction would help you better learn the subject?* The instructor is given the student feedback anonymously and during the following class session addresses the issues that are raised. The SGID does open up dialogue between instructors and students, but SGIDs are broadly focused and time-consuming. Few instructors are able to arrange for an SGID even once during a term and virtually none are able to have them more frequently.

Review of classroom videotapes, another way I have approached the problem, allows instructors to view and analyze both their performance and their students' behavior. It is very important for the students to be included in the taping because it often is the first time the instructors can actually *watch* how the students react during lectures and participate in discussions. Still, it does not create a dialogue between instructor and student.

My experience has shown that having graduate teaching assistants use Classroom Assessment Techniques (CATs) in structured assignments is the best way to develop their ability to look beyond their survival concerns by providing them with safe ways to engage their students in dialogues about learning.

Introducing Classroom Assessment to New Instructors

The semester-long *University Teaching Practicum* (FACDEV 2200) at the University of Pittsburgh is required for all College of Arts and Sciences teaching assistants and teaching fellows who will be teaching independently for the first time at Pitt, unless their department has received an exemption for a department-based course. Out of forty-three departments, only a few are exempted each term, usually those with a large number of TAs teaching recitations in large courses such as mathematics, English, and the international languages. In addition, several departments in the College of Arts and Sciences and departments in various professional schools (such as Pharmacy, Engineering, and Education) require their new teaching assistants or instructors to take the course during the first term they teach. Approximately eighty students each year have completed the course since I began teaching it in 1993.

The course currently meets for two hours each week of the term and carries 1 to 4 credit units. We have tried other formats in prior years, including meeting for the first seven weeks, taking a six-week break (during which the students are videotaped and have private consultations), and then meeting the final week of the term. The work is the same whether students register for one or four units; the variation is to allow students to register for their department-based course (for which we then give the grade) if it is required as part of their doctoral program, or to stay within funded credits.

In addition to the two CATs that students are required to complete (described later in this chapter), other assignments include being videotaped twice; writing analyses of their syllabi, student assignments, and student work; evaluating their own teaching and learning styles; writing a teaching philosophy and an "instructional script" (Grasha, 1996); and putting all their work together into a course portfolio (Cerbin, 1994).

FACDEV 2200 has a continuing focus on learning objectives. The students' first introduction to CATs is through the *teaching goals inventory* (Angelo and Cross, 1993), which they take within the first week of the course. Based on what they are trying to accomplish, the students design and implement two CATs, about five weeks apart. There are several steps in the structured CAT assignment:

> For each CAT you design and use, write and submit the following:
> 1. Description of the CAT; what are you trying to find out?
> 2. Describe your instructions to your students.
> 3. Attach the student feedback (the actual answers to the CAT).
> 4. What is your analysis of their answers?
> 5. Write a brief (1 page) description of how you responded to their answers, including how you discussed their answers with the students and how you will modify your teaching in response to what you found out.

Because the entire book of CATs (Angelo and Cross, 1993) can be overwhelming to new instructors, the FACDEV 2200 students are given a subset of three CATs (minute paper, categorizing grid, and background knowledge probe) to modify for their purposes. I also emphasize that CATs are useful for more than content. Table 8.2 shows the three CATs with examples focused on classroom culture and atmosphere and classroom process, as well as on content. In addition, we discuss the similarities and differences between CATs and tests and between CATs and end-of-term student evaluations.

Finding Instructors' Teaching Concerns. In our early discussions in FACDEV 2200, the students are asked about the courses they are teaching. As

Table 8.2. Examples of Three Types of CATs for Three Purposes

Type	Minute Paper	Categorizing Grid	Background Knowledge Probe
Classroom culture and atmosphere	What question would you have liked to ask in class today? Why didn't you ask it?	Which topics are you worried or uncomfortable about discussing in class? Comfortable Uncomfortable 1. women's rights 2. gun control 3. school integration 4. homosexuality	What have been your experiences in courses covering sensitive subjects? 1 = yes 2 = no __ students respectful __ students aware of other points of view __ comfortable with discussion
Classroom process	Describe your favorite ways of learning (for instance, discussion, field trips, library, debates, research papers).	Which teaching and learning techniques are helpful to you? Helpful Not Helpful 1. lecture 2. discussion 3. small groups 4. research projects 5. debate 6. field trips	What teaching and learning techniques have you used in previous courses? L = used a lot S = used some N = never used research paper small groups library project debates field trips
Content	What was the most important concept covered in class today?	This economic policy will affect which side of the economy? Demand Side Supply Side 1. reduction of federal income tax 2. airline deregulation 3. subsidized job training	Mark titles of plays you have encountered. R = read play T = saw on TV P = saw in theater W = worked in production __ As You Like It __ Oklahoma __ Hamlet __ Showboat

expected, they express teaching concerns such as those reported by Svinicki and others and noted in Table 8.1. Those teaching assistants who have never taught before mainly list concerns from Stage 1: *How can I get all the content covered? Will my lectures be clear enough? Will the students respect me? What if I can't answer students' questions? Will the students like me?* A smaller number of new TAs appear in the Prestage, with statements showing them to be in denial of their classroom responsibility and authority: *I just have to follow the department syllabus. The students will evaluate me on the department form; it must be OK. I am working hard on preparing my lectures (writing them out in detail).* Some of those who had prior teaching experience at other institutions expressed concerns at least partially in Stage 2: *How can I improve group discussions? How can I get the students to talk in class? How can I give clearer answers?* None of the FACDEV 2200 students, including those with considerable prior experience, have expressed Stage 3 concerns at the beginning of the course.

Doing the CATs. More than half of both new and experienced instructors have chosen to do a variation of the minute paper as their first CAT. (Until I required that the second CAT be a different structure from the first, many students did *two* minute papers.) The categorizing grid is a close runner-up, probably because by the time the students are ready to do their CATs it is too late in the term to do an overall-course background knowledge probe, although some do one for a new unit they are introducing. Most of the students are inventive with their CATs, understanding that a CAT must ask a question that is specific to the course and designed to give them information they need to improve their teaching. Very few students ask for the "what was the most important concept discussed today" generic minute paper.

Reacting to the CATs. The FACDEV 2200 students initially are not enthusiastic about having to interact so directly with their students, but they quickly find that breaking down the instructor-student barrier is not only useful but enjoyable:

> As a first-time teaching fellow, I was not looking forward, really, to doing a CAT and being criticized by the students early in the semester. However, I found it to be a great experience. It gave me an excellent opportunity to talk to my students on a more personal level. My class was an introductory one in my department and included a wide variety of student and experience levels. Many of the comments on the CATs were on the topic of the speed of the class; some thought I was going too slow; some too fast. So it gave me the chance to tell them about the diversity of the class. [Information Science]

> Once again I really enjoyed looking through my CAT results, and found the opportunity to give input into the class well used by my students. I know this is something I will continue to use throughout my teaching career. [Anthropology]

And in their end-of-term feedback the students have consistently rated the CAT assignments as "what helped my teaching the most." (The videotape analyses were second.)

Most important, the instructors' focus *after* their CATs was considerably more student-centered than when they were designing their CATs, showing movement along the developmental pathway toward concern with their students' learning. For instance, one teaching fellow designed a CAT to find out how well her students were remembering various ethical theories covered in the text and in discussion. Having analyzed the responses, she turned her attention away from concern about how she appeared ("being boring") to the students (Stage 1) to helping her students learn by showing them "how to break down a term into its components, to paraphrase it, so they could at least rule out one (or even two) of the theories as inappropriate headings" (Stage 2). A new teaching assistant found that the seeming "incorrect" responses on her categorizing grid CAT actually showed that her examples were open to interpretation (as well as confusion) by her students and decided that in the future she will include her CAT activity in the course itself, turning the focus from her "getting it right" (Stage 1) to helping students "learn to learn" (Stage 3). An experienced teaching fellow used a background knowledge probe to find out his students' familiarity with a wide variety of plays (Stage 2) in a world theater course in which he had both first-term freshmen and ready-to-graduate majors. He stated that "the feedback helped me gauge the 'point of entry' for most of the commonly read plays we will cover," which "also made me more sensitive to the needs of the 'intro' students, and how I need to take extra care of their progress and provide encouragement" (Stage 3).

A new teaching assistant who had returned to graduate school after a career in industry summed up the thoughts of many of his fellow students as follows:

> I found the use of CATs to be valuable not only to my understanding of my students, but surprisingly, noticed that the CATs themselves had a positive effect on student attitudes. Early this term, I asked my students to complete a CAT asking what they found most effective in class, and what they found least effective. Although their responses helped me modify my style in an attempt to be more effective vis-à-vis their learning, I also found that students appreciated the effort on my part. I could see it in their expressions, and heard it in their comments as we discussed the CAT in the lecture following its completion. I addressed the types of comments and gave my reaction as to each comment's appropriateness. It seemed the class lightened up a bit from that point forward. My second CAT this term was a categorization grid. We completed the grid and I collected the CATs. Immediately, I talked about the correct answers in an interactive format. The students seemed to really like the exercise, especially that I didn't just quiz them and drop the issue. They seemed to really appreciate not only the answers but also my explanations regarding the correct answers. In retrospect, it seems to me that the use of CATs is helpful to instructors; however, I was pleasantly surprised that subsequent discussions following the CATs were both productive and positive experiences for my students. I plan on duplicating these types of CATs, and their timing, in my classes in future semesters. [Computer Information Systems]

It is exactly that connection, the one that "lightens up" the class and creates "productive experiences" for the students, that I want to encourage as a primary goal for our developing instructors. Using CATs is the best way I have found to start that happening early in the teaching career.

References

Angelo, T. A., and Cross, K. P. *Classroom Assessment Techniques: A Handbook for College Teachers.* (2nd ed.) San Francisco: Jossey-Bass, 1993.

Cerbin, W. "The Course Portfolio as a Tool for Continuous Improvement of Teaching and Learning." *Journal on Excellence in College Teaching,* 1994, 5 (1), 95–105.

Fuller, F. F., and Brown, O. H. "Becoming a Teacher." In K. Ryan (ed.), *Teacher Education: The Seventy-Fourth Yearbook of the National Society for the Study of Education.* Vol. 2. Chicago: University of Chicago, 1975.

Grasha, A. F. *Teaching with Style.* Pittsburgh: Alliance, 1996.

Richlin, L. "Preparing the Faculty of the Future to Teach." In W. A. Wright and Associates, *Teaching Improvement Practices: Successful Strategies for Higher Education.* Bolton, Mass.: Anker, 1995.

Ronkowski, S. A. "Scholarly Teaching: Developmental Stages of Pedagogical Scholarship." In L. Richlin (ed.), *Preparing Faculty for the New Conceptions of Scholarship.* New Directions for Teaching and Learning, no. 54. San Francisco: Jossey-Bass, 1993.

Sprague, J., and Nyquist, J. D. "TA Supervision." In J. D. Nyquist, R. D. Abbott, and D. H. Wulff (eds.), *Teaching Assistant Training in the 1990s.* New Directions for Teaching and Learning, no. 39. San Francisco: Jossey-Bass, 1989.

Svinicki, M., Sullivan, T., Greer, M., and Diaz, M. "Combining Departmental Training with Central Support: A Research Project." Presented at Third National Conference on the Training and Employment of Graduate Teaching Assistants, Austin, Texas, Nov. 1991.

LAURIE RICHLIN is president of the International Alliance of Teacher Scholars, Pittsburgh, Pennsylvania.

Classroom Research can also assist in helping faculty understand the development of assessment for purposes beyond a single classroom.

Classroom Research and Program Accountability: A Match Made in Heaven?

Margaret Tebo-Messina, Chris Van Aller

"If you don't want to know, don't ask!" is a two-edged admonition. It simultaneously cautions and challenges classroom researchers. Beware, it says—those who conduct Classroom Assessment may find their illusions destroyed or discover they've not met student needs. Classroom Assessment is not for the timorous. It is for faculty concerned about student learning and serious about teaching. Dedicated researchers give students a chance to reveal what and how—and if—they are learning, without suffering reprisal. As a result these researchers' classes are invigorated and they develop professionally.

Accountability mandates are more Damoclean. Ever since *A Nation at Risk* (National Commission on Excellence in Education, 1983) indicted American education for contributing to the nation's social and economic ills, the public, the accrediting agencies, and the state governments have demanded that higher education prove its worth. Unfortunately, rather than cautioning, they threaten retribution. Increasingly assertive state legislators have closely examined higher education for areas of inefficiency, federal outlays for education have steadily declined, performance funding has become a reality, the bastion of tenure is under siege, and the threat of national standards is omnipresent. The drive for educational reform has become a stampede. . . .

No wonder faculty resist and resent accountability mandates. Identifying individual weaknesses at the classroom or institutional level is one thing, public confession quite another. In the first instance, assessment is *formative*; it propels ongoing processes of evaluation and improvement. It means reflecting and adjusting and refocusing so as to do a better job and then once again gathering evidence. In the second instance, however, assessment is *summative*—it passes judgment. It means submitting required data to some external authority with funding or validating power. Although the overriding concern of both types of assessment is the quality of higher education, they operate quite differently. They are as unlikely a pair as private rumination and public declamation, as Emily Dickinson and Ralph Nader. But Winthrop University has mated Classroom Research and program accountability in its Learning Research Project (LRP), which focuses on general education skills and abilities. The union has at times been difficult. As with any long-term relationship, it has required adaptation, compromise, perseverance, encouragement, and support.

Winthrop University's Response to the Challenge

Winthrop is a state-supported comprehensive institution of about 5,500 students, most of whom come from South Carolina and surrounding states. Increasingly achievement-oriented and diverse, the undergraduate student body includes approximately 23 percent older returning students, more than 25 percent minorities, and many first-generation college students. The challenges of teaching such a diverse group are formidable, especially as Winthrop is dedicated to fostering a wide range of general education skills and abilities.

Like other colleges and universities in South Carolina, Winthrop falls under the jurisdiction of the Southern Association of Colleges and Schools (SACS). In addition to responding to the SACS assessment requirements, Winthrop, like other public institutions, is required by state law to assess nineteen components of campus life—everything from advising to zoology, library services to administrative operations and, of course, general education. A 1998 "cutting edge" legislative mandate requires that yearly Institutional Effectiveness Plans and Reports be sent to the state's Commission on Higher Education (and ultimately to the legislature), detailing assessment methods and results. While its intention is to promote self-examination and improvement, subsequent legislation requires reported data to be arrayed in matrices to facilitate institutional comparisons.

Fortunately, neither state nor SACS mandates prescribe *how* to assess: institutions are free to design methods appropriate to their unique situation. Nevertheless, our faculty's reactions to assessment have ranged from paranoid muttering about hidden agendas to ostrichlike indifference to grudging and cautious acceptance of the inevitable. Even faculty who recognized their responsibility for the quality of higher education and for Winthrop's general education program have often viewed assessment as an added burden.

Thanks to the foresight and determination of a small but dedicated group of faculty and administrators, Winthrop has become a leader in the assessment movement. In 1988 the university established an Office of Assessment, staffed by a faculty director of assessment and faculty coordinator of general education assessment (both of whom teach half-time), and, to ensure representation of various academic units and committees, it created a faculty Assessment Advisory Board.

The board endorsed these "General Principles" to guide Winthrop's assessment efforts[1]:

1. The primary reason for assessment is to improve student learning and development.
2. The assessment program is designed primarily for internal decision making to improve programs, instruction, and related services.
3. Assessment program initiatives must include training and related resources for faculty and student support personnel responsible for assessment activities.
4. Faculty participation in student assessment activities will be appropriately supported and recognized by the university.
5. Developing an effective, valid assessment program is a long-term, dynamic process.
6. The assessment program will seek to use the most reliable, valid methods and instruments.
7. Assessment must involve a multimethod approach.
8. The technical limitations of data will be considered during subsequent decision making and delineated in reports.
9. Assessment results are not intended to be used punitively against students.
10. Assessment of student learning and development is a process that is distinct from faculty evaluation.

Philosophically, Winthrop has taken a quiet approach to accountability—one more in keeping with Emily Dickinson than with Ralph Nader. Its emphasis on assessment for internal improvement and its insistence on faculty decision making and participation recognize that the processes of exploring and reflecting and gathering evidence must be very personal experiences if they are to be meaningful.

From the very beginning of its assessment efforts, the university has been sensitive to the fact that the average harried faculty member, especially if not yet tenured, is under increasing pressure not only to publish but to participate in a host of campus activities and to excel as a teacher. Consequently, the university adopted guidelines for crediting faculty work in assessment as teaching, scholarship, or service.

General Education at Winthrop University

In 1993, Winthrop faculty concluded a two-year process to clarify the intent of their ten-year-old general education goals, and to articulate more concrete and measurable objectives in each area. The dialogue that occurred was important for several reasons. It heightened our collective awareness of general education and, more important for the interdisciplinary nature of the LRP, it brought to light the fact that Winthrop faculty believe the entire university experience, that is, *all* courses and activities, should help develop these skills and abilities. Whether or not one teaches a designated course, one still has a "general education responsibility." Yet because general education is everyone's responsibility and really the core of our type of institution, assessing it must be an interdisciplinary endeavor.

The Learning Research Project

The idea of using Classroom Research as a major component of general education program assessment grew along with the frustration of the Office of Assessment faculty. The program data collected from student and alumni surveys and standardized commercial tests were having little impact on those general education courses. And efforts to engage faculty in developing home-grown general education assessment measures—except in the area of writing—were unsuccessful. The director and coordinator realized that assessment methods divorced from the classroom had little likelihood of fostering growth, quality, or any needed change in general education. In *assessmentese* there was no direct way of "closing the loop" between aggregate data and general education, between abstract numbers and what happened in a hundred or more courses. Although the assessment measures were satisfying current external accountability mandates, they did not meet Winthrop's internal mandate that assessment must lead to improved learning.

Classroom Research, on the other hand, had the potential to improve learning, interest faculty, and satisfy external demands. Despite design drawbacks inherent in the Classroom Research process, the director and coordinator were optimistic, idealistic, and frankly naive about the real challenges they would face.

The next step was to seek input from faculty on the Assessment Advisory Board. Despite the problems they foresaw, everyone agreed that if faculty got involved in the LRP, they could get immediate payback in their classrooms. They would understand that assessment might result in personal rewards as well as some of that statistical information so dear to bureaucrats everywhere. But could faculty be convinced to participate? Would they consider assessing general education goals relevant even in courses not part of general education? Would they be willing to spend time exploring how well or if their students learned those skills and abilities? Would the data obtained lend itself to substantive reports for the external examiners and satisfy our internal critics as well?

Tentative Beginnings. To answer these questions, the Learning Research Project was piloted during the 1990–91 academic year. It called for recruiting and training faculty each semester in the use of Classroom Assessment Techniques, asking for a three-semester commitment in return for training, materials, and a modest travel stipend. Participants would sign contracts agreeing to the following steps:

1. Adapt or create Classroom Assessment Techniques that gather data on the seven goals of general education.
2. Develop reporting mechanisms that make it possible to publish results on campus and in periodic reports to the Commission on Higher Education, while simultaneously preserving researchers' anonymity.
3. Foster the use of Classroom Assessment Techniques as a faculty-driven and controlled means of assessment.
4. Take an active part in evaluating, brainstorming, and planning the project's future direction.
5. Participate in introductory workshops, follow-up sessions, and team meetings.
6. Discuss progress and problems informally with other researchers and a coordinator as needed but at least every other week while conducting Classroom Assessment.
7. Promote learning research on campus and recruit new faculty participants.
8. Write a detailed report evaluating the experience with Classroom Assessment Techniques.

The initial plan included two day-long training workshops, relaxed affairs at the coordinator's home with plenty of food available. It also called for five gatherings during the semester and bi-weekly informal drop-in lunches at the student center.

The coordinators also devised an end-of-semester reporting format based on their recent Berkeley training in Classroom Research (Brooks, Angelo, and Cross, 1990, p. 118) that asked participants to provide quantitative data whenever possible in answer to the following questions:

1. How many students were in your target class? What level students were they?
2. Approximately how many hours did you spend on the project? In class? Outside of class analyzing and interpreting information?
3. How many assessment techniques did you use?
4. Did you change anything that you normally do in this class because of the information your assessment efforts yielded?
5. If so, what effect did the change have on you? On your students?
6. Will you do anything differently the next time you teach this course?
7. Did your assessment efforts bear in any way on Winthrop's general education goals? Which goals? What hypothesis or conclusion did you come to about student attainment of those goals?
8. Have you done any presentation or written any articles pertaining to learning research?
9. What surprised you most in doing Classroom Assessment?
10. What have been the most enjoyable aspects of the project? The least enjoyable?

It was made clear to participants that any summary reports produced by the Office of Assessment would protect their anonymity.

The Pilot Project. During the fall of 1990, nine faculty recruits were trained in the use of Classroom Assessment Techniques. The second semester, the coordinator and these nine recruited additional researchers or wooed faculty from disciplines that offered general education courses. By the end of 1991, seventeen faculty members—representing art and design, business administration, art history, education, English, the library, mass communication, mathematics, political science, psychology, sociology, social work, and speech—had joined the project. They had been urged to spend their first semester trying out a few simple techniques before focusing specifically on general education goals.

Pilot Project Results. A summary of 1990–91 reports shows that collectively the LRP had assessed and improved the learning of almost half of Winthrop's undergraduate student body, over two thousand individuals. Faculty had experimented with more than fifteen different assessment techniques and developed or modified some of their own. One inspired example is the *one minute drawing,* a variation of the minute paper (Angelo and Cross, 1993, p. 148), designed to get immediate visual feedback from art history students. After a slide-lecture, the professor might, for example, ask students to sketch Corinthian, Doric, and Ionic columns. The repeated use of this technique served at least two purposes: the teacher knew quickly whether her students had "gotten it," and her requests emphasized the importance of key constructs.

The information gleaned from Classroom Assessment Techniques was often disconcerting. Faculty found, for example, that students "[did] not always hear what I thought they were hearing;" that "[they] were not recalling as much content information as I thought." Researchers responded to their discoveries by modifying their teaching in the target classes: they increased class time devoted to skill learning, modeled expected behaviors, and even included required self-assessments. The end result of all this self-examination and experimentation was improvement—95 percent of the LRP faculty reported seeing a definite increase in their students' learning. In one sociology class, for example, the proportion of students capable of "integrating information from various sources" increased from 22 percent to 75 percent.

There were rewards outside the classroom as well—collegiality, conference presentations, better student evaluations. Faculty were realizing that assessment could help advance their careers and satisfy the institution as well. As Tom Angelo put it at a recent assessment conference, the bottom line is that this research is becoming more accepted as equivalent to that in the discipline, particularly in state institutions with high teaching loads and ever-higher demands in terms of accountability, larger classes, and higher graduation rates.

With success came unforeseen problems: as the LRP grew in size so too did the time strain on the coordinators. It was becoming difficult to sustain the interdisciplinary dynamic that created so much energy and enthusiasm.

Somehow the energizing and instructive effects of small groups had to be retained and perhaps refined.

Most important, despite the demonstrated benefits of Classroom Assessment for individual faculty, they and the project leaders realized that the LRP had to be more deliberately focused on general education. The first stage had produced wonderful improvements in many classrooms, but too few general education goals had been assessed in too cursory a manner to have program relevance. A second phase was needed.

Learning Research Project Phase II

The first step was to come up with a new structure. The following plan was worked out by the project coordinators and faculty researchers to address the issues noted in the preceding section:

- The LRP will be broken down into three of four smaller teams, each charged with assessing a particular general education goal. Each team leader will be an experienced and dedicated researcher.
- Teams, or their individual members, will be free to assess additional questions or goals (either personal or related to the general education goals), but must collectively address the goal of their chosen team.
- Individual faculty will still determine what kind of assessments and research to do in their classes.
- However, teams will explore how or if particular techniques are especially suited to assessing certain goals, or goals in specific disciplines.
- The project will be coordinated by the team leaders, the coordinator of general education assessment, and the director of the Office of Assessment. They will train new researchers, recruit faculty, coordinate teams, develop future plans, and monitor project results.
- The entire LRP faculty will meet twice a semester; teams will meet at least two additional times. At the semester's final meeting, teams will present findings for discussion.

A decision was also made to publicize the LRP and disseminate its findings and recommendations in campus publications, at faculty meetings, and in reports to the general education governing committee. In addition, administrators were invited to year-end meetings.

Implementing the New Plan. To begin, LRP faculty were asked to prioritize the seven general education goals in terms of their research interests. Their initial choices—communication, quantitative skills, and aesthetic appreciation—determined each team's focus. The project coordinators approached committed veterans to take on team leadership in hopes that the work of energizing and caring for the project could be shared.

A deliberate effort was made to draw recruits from new disciplines, especially from departments with substantial general education course offerings.

The desire to retain the interdisciplinary nature of the project and of each team created new logistical problems. The more diverse the groups became, the more difficult it was to schedule training sessions and meeting times.

Everything possible was done to fit the schedules of new recruits. The coordinators also drew heavily on the expertise of veteran researchers to help address a recurring problem: new recruits tended to design massive projects and have trouble overcoming their discipline's research paradigm. They often started planning dependent and independent variables, control groups, and statistical procedures. Fortunately, the old-timers in the group could usually guide them in more productive directions.

Most groups would come to appreciate that the mating of Classroom Assessment and accountability could be productive. What Cross (1990, pp. 82–83) has called the ancestors of Classroom Research—faculty development, assessment, educational research—were, in fact, the offspring of the LRP.

Despite, or perhaps because of, its insistent focus on student learning, the LRP became a place where faculty seriously grappled with pedagogical concerns. Conversations would often begin with one researcher sharing a particularly painful or illuminating insight gained from an assessment technique. Gradually, researchers from other disciplines would contribute similar insights—an English professor's realization that her honor students could not paraphrase material extended a psychology professor's realization that his students either thought too globally or too concretely—and sometimes a teaching or research hypothesis was born. This teacher-talk differed in kind from casual story swapping in the faculty lounge. For one thing, it was interdisciplinary—but more important, it was based on systematic and thoughtful analysis of assessment results.

As for assessment—the *Big A* type of institutional or program level accountability—the LRP's progeny exhibited remarkable similarities. Its collective focus on general education goals stretched the horizons of individual researchers: they were simultaneously concerned with very course-specific learning and with skills and abilities that transcended departmental boundaries. The team approach enlarged the scale of the project and made comparing various curricular and pedagogical approaches inevitable and easy, and public. Admittedly, the majority of data gathered never left campus and were never used *summatively,* but they were influencing Winthrop's view of general education.

One Team's Story. The most successful learning research group to date has been the Aesthetic Team, which concentrated on assessing student ability "To understand aesthetic values, the creative process, and the interconnectedness of the literary, visual, and performing arts." Ironically, this team tackled a goal that was arguably the most challenging to operationalize and quantify. Despite its difficult charge and small size, or perhaps because of them, this team remained dynamic and energetic during its three-year pursuit of a Winthrop-specific approach to assessing aesthetic appreciation. Although group members changed over the years, a core group and the team leader never changed. This stability had much to do with the team's success.

The team members started by learning to talk and understand one another's languages and by developing a common understanding of aesthetic values, which broadened their disciplinary perspectives. They spent the 1993 spring semester discussing, doing literature searches, brainstorming, and soul-searching, and as they narrowed in on their research question, the members all took turns outlining how metaphor was used in their disciplines. Finally they agreed on the following rationale: "The creative process has been defined as the ability to make new and significant connections between two seemingly unrelated ideas: objects and events. This definition parallels the concept of metaphor as the understanding and experiencing of one kind of thing in terms of another. . . . Both the maker and the interpreter of art are engaged in a metaphoric process" (Aesthetic Team, 1994).

And they posed the following research question: *Do students demonstrate an understanding of how metaphor is used in various disciplines?*

After two and a half years, the team's assessment measure neared completion. They had met dozens of times each academic year and even during the summer to pilot test measures, develop exercises, select readings, write a script, and create a videotape illustrating metaphor in poetry, music, dance, and the visual arts. Their multimedia plan now includes a video to introduce students to the uses of metaphor, instructor-led course-specific discussions of metaphor, and then assessment of student understanding using a variation of the annotated portfolio technique (Angelo and Cross, 1993, p. 208). Finally, students are assigned a discipline-specific project requiring the use of metaphor.

Phase II Results. Over the next three years, the LRP began to sell itself. Faculty actually sought out the program. Why? For one thing, the many useful and effective assessment strategies contained in the first Cross and Angelo edition had proved their utility over a wide range of subjects. Minute papers and goal ranking (Angelo and Cross, 1993, p. 290) were used in ballet and business courses, speech and elementary education courses, introductory science courses, library and English courses. Some were adapted in intriguing and innovative ways to each teaching situation. In a Theatre Practicum, for example, goal ranking was modified into a three-part assessment administered before, during, and after a stage production:

Part I: A questionnaire was given to student actors preparing a faculty-directed production of *Reckless*. It sought feedback on the actor's feelings about auditions and the part in which he or she was cast; the actor's personal goals for the production; and the actor's ideas of the collective goal—what might be achieved by the ensemble as a whole.

Part II: Halfway through the production the questionnaire was returned and the actors were asked to evaluate their progress toward their individual goals and their sense of the progress on the collective goal.

Part III: The Monday following the close of the play, the questionnaire was returned and the actors wrote a final evaluation of the goals and their progress. At this time about an hour was spent in group discussion reflecting on the shared creative process—what was good and what could be done to improve future productions (Personal communication, Jeannie M. Woods, Aesthetic Team member, 1994).

The teacher reported that "the questionnaire alerted [her] to potential problems and stress points which [she] might otherwise have missed."

The team meetings produced remarkable dialogues on the benefits of using such techniques in the classroom, dialogues that not only refined each researcher's thinking but gave all a much-needed inspirational shot in the arm. The meetings became one of the very few series that people actually looked forward to.

Unfortunately, finances restricted the project's growth somewhat. The project's budget was shrinking. Winthrop was not the culprit: the state had reduced outlays to higher education in unprecedented proportions. But the Office of Assessment director and the coordinator of General Education Assessment insisted on recognizing faculty contributions not only with materials but with money. Although the travel stipend was too small to be much of a drawing card and many faculty never used it, money communicated administrative support.

Despite the budget strain, by the end of the fifth year over 25 percent of Winthrop full-time faculty had been involved in the LRP and 75 percent of those chose to stay on beyond their three-semester commitment. These facts suggest that the project was rewarding in and of itself. The LRP had achieved critical mass.

New Problems. Although most of the teams experienced stimulating and fruitful discussions, most also experienced real frustrations. One found it impossible to arrive at a mutually agreeable approach to researching their chosen goal, communication. This may have been due to the genuinely difficult nature of interdisciplinary research, to the complexity of their goal, to leadership, or a concatenation of problems. Eventually the team disbanded: some researchers left the project, some moved to other goal teams, and a few volunteered to head up a new project to assess oral communication skills.

The Diversity Team (formed in 1994), on the other hand, approached its goal with such fervor that attempts to agree on the meaning of *diversity* became heated debates. Their "problem" was a cognizance of the far-reaching effect their recommendations might have, a concern that eventually their work would reach well beyond the parameters of the general education curriculum. However, their efforts were not wasted and continue today: in fact, their struggles give flesh to the assessment truism that the process is often, if not always, more important than the product. While the team remains very much in a discussion and experimental mode, their initial work has both helped heighten interest in the goal and provide a way for Winthrop to begin to assess diversity awareness, a most vital issue for a campus with over 25 percent African American students.

Of course, team leaders sometimes found it difficult to overcome disciplinary compartmentalization and to negotiate between strong egos. The project coordinators therefore have since concentrated on finding those people who, like Eisenhower with his generals before D-Day, can keep strong personalities working together on long-term goals.

Sometimes the measurement methods developed were inadequate. A case in point—one team devised a "math" instrument to assess students' levels of competence not only in mathematics and the physical sciences but in any course where quantitative skills were important. One popular biology professor, a highly respected and dynamic teacher, found in a pre/post pilot test that his students scored lower the second time they were assessed! Although the team continued to refine the instrument, they also began asking questions about curriculum and pedagogy—further indication that assessment and Classroom Research are evolutionary but positive endeavors.

Yet another issue that arose was how to convince new recruits to buy into the philosophy and purpose of the LRP. One group in particular had several members who were very interested in improving their teaching and very uninterested in accountability. Effective leadership helped convince these souls that documenting their work would simultaneously benefit the institution and help them accomplish their professional goals.

Indeed, the scholarly work coming out of the LRP was and is very convincing: researchers have not only done presentations in their departments and conducted workshops for other South Carolina institutions, they have exported Classroom Research to institutions in China and Australia, given more than twenty presentations at regional and national conferences, and published more than fifteen journal articles based on their use of Classroom Assessment Techniques.

Final Thoughts

On a personal note, the authors have to confess that we're addicted to Classroom Research, that we use Classroom Assessment Techniques constantly, that we don't know how we ever taught without them. The LRP has invigorated our teaching and given us the opportunity to share with colleagues in a variety of disciplines.

What's more, the LRP has convinced us that Classroom Research and accountability make a fecund couple: the intrinsic energy and dynamism of Classroom Research can overcome faculty aversion to assessment; the inherent challenges and rewards of Classroom Assessment can nourish program-level assessment. But it takes time and determination and patience. We'd like to sum up our hard-learned lessons.

Starting the Project. Looking back, we believe that seeking input from administration and faculty advisory boards before beginning was a smart move. We got their support—both dollars and encouragement—and kept it even during rough times because we took time to explain how the context-specific nature of Classroom Research made it adaptable to our campus culture and mission. We pointed out that Winthrop's general education program would only improve when faculty from all across campus were involved in its assessment. Instead of stressing accountability demands, we emphasized student learning.

Engaging and Retaining Faculty. We learned that when assessment is focused on issues faculty care about—namely learning and teaching—they will come. They will come if encouraged to address their own teaching questions and goals before working on program-level questions. And, although Classroom Research is intrinsically rewarding, faculty—especially untenured faculty—are more likely to stay in a project if the institution acknowledges (and values) the professionalism of the activity. Because Winthrop administration has agreed that faculty work in assessment may and should receive credit as teaching, scholarship, or service, LRP work appears in faculty annual reports and tenure and promotion dossiers.

It also appears in campus publicity and required public reports—but in summary form. Protecting the privacy and anonymity of faculty researchers builds trust and leads to more openness, spontaneity, and intellectual growth.

Other more immediate and tangible rewards also help. Money, for example. Even when modest, funds for training and travel affirm the importance of assessment. Letters from project directors acknowledging individual contributions are also encouraging. And food—at meetings and training sessions—is a must.

Sustaining the Energy. The LRP's long-term survival has required lots of conversation—small group and large group meetings have been all-important in building rapport and extending our individual vision. However, committed leadership at all levels seems to have been the key determiner of the project's success (and its failures). Team leaders, for example, not only had to arrange plenty of meeting times and keep their groups motivated, they had to facilitate interdisciplinary discussions. Although such exchanges could (and usually did) further everyone's thinking, they could also "fail" to overcome individual research and scholarship biases. Project leaders, we discovered, needed energy, enthusiasm, an overabundance of listening skills, and lots of patience. Those qualities enabled group members to hear and understand one another's language, to articulate their own intellectually relevant research questions, to keep going despite the workload.

In sum, Winthrop's experience with Classroom Research has been well worth the frustrations endured, the energy and effort expended, and the time spent. Although the LRP has much left to accomplish in terms of program assessment, its impact on our campus has been profound. Every school on campus—and virtually every department—has active classroom researchers. Their energy, enthusiasm, and commitment bode well for this unlikely mating. Dickinson and Nader may not be such an odd couple after all.

Note

1. Material drawn from internal documents and printed with permission of Office of Assessment, Winthrop University.

References

Aesthetic Team, unpublished report, 1994.

Angelo, T. A., and Cross, K. P. *Classroom Assessment Techniques: A Handbook for College Teachers.* (2nd ed.) San Francisco: Jossey-Bass, 1993.

Brooks, K. O., Angelo, T. A., and Cross, K. P. *Classroom Research: A Manual for Campus Coordinators.* Berkeley: University of California Press, 1990.

Cross, K. P. "Intermediate Classroom Research 102." Paper presented at the Workshop in Classroom Research. University of California, Berkeley, June 13, 1990.

National Commission on Excellence in Education. *A Nation at Risk.* Washington, D.C.: U.S. Department of Education, 1983.

MARGARET TEBO-MESSINA, professor of English at Winthrop University, is the former coordinator of general education assessment who initiated the Learning Research Project (LRP). Currently she is executive director of the South Carolina Higher Education Assessment Network.

CHRIS VAN ALLER, associate professor of political science at Winthrop University, is a long-time member of the LRP. Currently, he is coleader of the Diversity Team.

Classroom Assessment can be modified to serve the development of student teams when group collaboration is a goal of the course.

A Collective Effort Classroom Assessment Technique: Promoting High Performance in Student Teams

Charles Walker, Thomas Angelo

Why don't more college instructors teach students how to work in teams? Most instructors realize when they ask students to write about the Civil War west of the Mississippi or the fuzzy logic of love, they must also teach writing. Likewise, when instructors ask students to make oral presentations on web strumming mimicry in Portia spiders, they must also teach speaking. However, fewer instructors have the insight that when they ask students to work in groups, they must also teach students how to work as a team, or what might be called *teaming.*

Probably a major reason why teaming is not taught as earnestly as other skills is because most instructors do not know as much about group structures and processes as they do about writing or speaking. This lack of knowledge about groups is certainly not a shortcoming restricted to historians, mathematicians, or biologists; until lately, even social scientists were vexed by the peculiarities of group behavior. However, in recent years, promising new research on group performance has been published that will not only help us understand groups better, it should also help us design better methods to teach and promote teaming. In this chapter we will summarize this research and describe a new assessment technique for guiding and monitoring student teams.

Note: Part of the research reported in this article was first presented at the national convention of the American Psychological Association held in Chicago in August 1997. Correspondence and inquiries should be directed to Charles Walker, Department of Psychology, St. Bonaventure University, St. Bonaventure, NY 14778.

Practice-Based Wisdom on Using Groups

Although collaborative learning is still on the fringe of higher education, interest in it has risen significantly (Bruffee, 1993; Smith, Johnson, and Johnson, 1992). Even without the benefit of basic research, many instructors have discovered on their own what works and what doesn't with student groups. For example, Slavin (1990) found that student groups perform best when they have common goals, joint rewards, and ways to make sure individuals are accountable. To obtain positive outcomes like improving the quality of student interactions, getting students to use higher-order thinking skills, or increasing their interest in learning, Cooper and Mueck (1992) recommend that instructors highly structure group assignments and provide sufficient in-class time for groups to do their work. Fiechtner and Davis (1985), on the other hand, recommend what not to do. They urge instructors not to allow students to form their own groups, minimize the effect group performance has on grades, leave out peer evaluation, or assign group tasks that can be done alone by individuals. However, with notable exceptions (Michaelson and Black, 1994; Walker, 1995), despite what we have learned about what does and does not work with groups, most instructors still report having problems with student motivation, or what has been called free riding. Free riding is a form of social loafing seen in a group when one or more members slack off and "ride" on the extra efforts of their coworkers (Johnson, Johnson, and Holubec, 1990). Gamson (1994) proposed that to solve problems like free riding, instructors must find useful theories on group performance. We believe we have found one such theory. In the next sections, we will summarize this new theory and discuss its implications for teaching and assessing teaming.

Results of Basic Research on Social Loafing

For over a century, social psychologists have been studying the effects groups have on the performance of individuals. In fact, some of the first researchers in social psychology (Kravitz and Martin, 1986) sought answers to the same questions that now befuddle many instructors who use groups in their classrooms: when does working with others enhance performance and when does it detract from performance? Because of a rebirth of interest in this topic, since 1965 hundreds of studies have been conducted on social loafing and social facilitation. What was unclear and perplexing about group performance only a couple decades ago is now much better understood. In a recent review of this literature, Karau and Williams (1995) conclude that social loafing is decreased when:

- The work of individuals can be evaluated by themselves or others.
- Individuals' contributions to the group are unique.
- Individuals know what good performance is for the group and themselves.
- The work of the group is seen as important and meaningful.
- The group's task can not be easily done by a single individual.

- Groups are smaller ($N < 7$).
- Group members have mutual respect.
- Each member values working in a collective.

A Model for the Promotion of Collective Effort

After summarizing the research on group performance, Karau and Williams proposed a new model of collective effort, a model that should be of interest to instructors who wish to teach teaming. Their model combines elements from expectancy-value theories with those from social-identity and social-comparison theories (Abrams and Hogg, 1990; Goethals and Darley, 1987). Karau and Williams suggest that individuals will work harder in groups when they believe a group can achieve an outcome and the outcome is extrinsically or intrinsically valuable. According to Karau and Williams, two important things are at stake for students when they join a group: their *sense of efficacy,* which may be strengthened or weakened, and their *social identity,* which may be affirmed or contested. When students exert effort, they must believe that this work will be instrumental to the group's achieving outcomes that are valuable both to the group and themselves. However, the satisfactory achievement of valued outcomes such as solving complex real-world problems may not be enough to guarantee high levels of effort from all group members. Students also need to learn about themselves and feel validated; to promote self-development, the *unique* contribution of each student must be recognized and evaluated fairly by competent, respected coworkers.

While the formula for stimulating high levels of effort and achievement in student groups is simple, it is quite challenging to implement in practice. An assessment device or instrument to monitor student groups would be helpful, not only to promote high group performance, but also to help instructors teach teaming and students learn how to work in groups. In the final part of this chapter we will describe a new Classroom Assessment Technique for enhancing collective effort, give evidence on its effectiveness, and suggest ways to use it.

A Method for the Assessment of Collective Effort

The purpose of the Collective Effort Classroom Assessment Technique (CECAT) is to stimulate the healthy development of student groups. It is designed to be used with student groups that will work together for an extended period of time (half a semester or longer). It can be used with project groups, committees, applied problem-solving teams, case study teams, or other collaborative or cooperative teams. If the CECAT is used as recommended, it should help students avoid the detrimental consequences of social loafing (that is, free riding) while stimulating them to perform highly both as individuals and as a group. Exhibits 10.1, 10.2, and 10.3 present *early, midway,* and *summative* versions of the CECAT. In Exhibit 10.4 the CECAT items have been sorted into group structure and group process categories for the convenience of instructors who wish to design their own instruments.

Exhibit 10.1. An Early Assessment of Group Work

Please indicate your level of agreement with each of the following statements using a five-point agree-disagree rating scale, where 1 = strongly disagree, 2 = disagree, 3 = uncertain, 4 = agree, and 5 = strongly agree (the higher the number, the more you agree).

1. _____ My group will perform excellently.
2. _____ All the members of the group will work equally hard.
3. _____ As our work progresses, the group should become more cohesive.
4. _____ I want to feel proud of my group and I desire to work with people I highly respect.
5. _____ Most of the members of the group appear to value working in a collective with others.
6. _____ What the group will try to achieve is valuable and important to other members of the group.
7. _____ What the group will try to achieve is valuable and important to me.
8. _____ The group's task is intrinsically interesting.
9. _____ Other members of my group will not only know what I am doing, they will easily *see* what I am doing to monitor my work.
10. _____ Performance standards for the group will be set to allow us to evaluate the overall performance of the entire group as we work.
11. _____ The group I will be working in is just the right size.
12. _____ Performance standards for individuals will be set to allow each person to evaluate his or her contribution while he or she works for the group.
13. _____ The effort I exert will be instrumental in helping me obtain outcomes I want to achieve as an individual.
14. _____ My performance will be evaluated by the instructor or by other members of my group.
15. _____ The task of the group will require all of us to meet and work side by side, face to face, most of the time.
16. _____ I will exert a lot of effort to help the group achieve its goals.
17. _____ I have a lot of things to contribute to the group's work such as knowledge, skill, effort, time, and other essentials.
18. _____ My performance as an individual will directly affect how well the group as a whole will perform.
19. _____ My contribution to the group's work is unique; no one else will be doing exactly what I'm doing.
20. _____ The task of the group will be challenging.

_____ Total score

Exhibit 10.2. A Midway Assessment of Group Work

Please indicate your level of agreement with each of the following statements using a five-point agree-disagree rating scale, where 1 = strongly disagree, 2 = disagree, 3 = uncertain, 4 = agree, and 5 = strongly agree (the higher the number, the more you agree).

1. _____ My group is performing excellently.
2. _____ All the members of the group are working equally hard.
3. _____ As our work progresses, the group is becoming more cohesive.
4. _____ I am proud to be a member of the group and I highly respect most of the people I am working with.
5. _____ Most of the members of the group highly value working in a collective with others.
6. _____ What the group is trying to achieve is valuable and important to other members of the group.
7. _____ What the group is trying to achieve is valuable and important to me.
8. _____ The group's task is intrinsically interesting.
9. _____ Other members of my group not only know what I am doing, they can easily *see* what I am doing and monitor my work.
10. _____ Performance standards for the group have been set to allow us to evaluate the overall performance of the entire group as we are working.
11. _____ The group I am working in is just the right size.
12. _____ Performance standards for individuals have been set to allow each person to evaluate his or her contribution to the group.
13. _____ The effort I have exerted thus far has been instrumental in helping me obtain outcomes I want to achieve as an individual.
14. _____ My performance is being (or will be) evaluated by the instructor or by other members of my group.
15. _____ The task of the group requires all of us to meet and work side by side, face to face, most of the time.
16. _____ I am exerting a lot of effort to help the group achieve its goals.
17. _____ I am contributing a lot of things to the group's work such as knowledge, skill, effort, time, and other essentials.
18. _____ My performance as an individual is directly affecting how well the group as a whole performs.
19. _____ My contribution to the group's work is unique; no one else is doing exactly what I'm doing.
20. _____ The task of the group is challenging.

_____ Total score

Exhibit 10.3. A Summative Assessment of Group Work

Please indicate your level of agreement with each of the following statements using a five-point agree-disagree rating scale, where 1 = strongly disagree, 2 = disagree, 3 = uncertain, 4 = agree, and 5 = strongly agree (the higher the number, the more you agree).

1. _____ My group performed excellently.
2. _____ All the members of the group worked equally hard.
3. _____ As our work progressed, the group became more cohesive.
4. _____ I was proud to be a member of the group and I highly respected most of the people I worked with.
5. _____ Most of the members of the group highly valued working in a collective with others.
6. _____ What the group achieved (or tried to achieve) was considered important and valuable to other members of the group.
7. _____ What the group achieved (or tried to achieve) was valuable and important to me.
8. _____ The group's task was intrinsically interesting.
9. _____ Other members of my group not only knew what I was doing, they could easily see what I was doing and monitor my work.
10. _____ Performance standards for the group were set in advance to allow us to evaluate the overall performance of the entire group as we worked.
11. _____ The group I worked in was just the right size.
12. _____ Performance standards for individuals were set in advance to allow each person to evaluate his or her contribution while he or she worked for the group.
13. _____ The effort I exerted was instrumental in helping me obtain the outcomes I wanted to achieve as an individual.
14. _____ My performance was evaluated by the instructor or by other members of my group.
15. _____ The task of the group required us to meet and work side by side most of the time; we did not work alone and then combine our efforts only at the end.
16. _____ I exerted a lot of effort to help the group achieve its goals.
17. _____ I had a lot of things to contribute to the group's work such as knowledge, skill, effort, time, and other essentials.
18. _____ My performance as an individual directly affected how well the group as a whole performed.
19. _____ My contribution to the group's work was unique; no one else did exactly what I did.
20. _____ The task of the group was challenging.

_____ Total score

Exhibit 10.4. CECAT Items Sorted by Their Social Function

Group Composition

I am proud to be a member of the group and I highly respect most of the people I am working with.

I am contributing a lot of things to the group's work such as knowledge, skill, effort, time, and other essentials.

Most of the members of the group highly value working in a collective with others.

The group I am working in is just the right size.

Task Characteristics

The group's task is intrinsically interesting.

The task of the group is challenging.

The task of the group requires all of us to meet and work side by side, face to face, most of the time.

Processes and Procedures

My contribution to the group's work is unique; no one else is doing exactly what I'm doing.

Other members of my group not only know what I am doing, they can easily *see* what I am doing and monitor my work.

My performance as an individual is directly affecting how well the group as a whole performs.

Individual and Group Motivation

What the group is trying to achieve is valuable and important to other members of the group.

What the group is trying to achieve is valuable and important to me.

All the members of the group are working equally hard.

The effort I have exerted thus far has been instrumental in helping me obtain outcomes I want to achieve as an individual.

Performance Evaluation

Performance standards for the group have been set to allow us to evaluate the overall performance of the entire group as we are working.

Performance standards for individuals have been set to allow each person to evaluate his or her contribution to the group.

My performance is being (or will be) evaluated by the instructor or by other members of my group.

General Conditions and Outcomes

My group is performing excellently.

As our work progresses, the group is becoming more cohesive.

I am exerting a lot of effort to help the group achieve its goals.

Validation of the CECAT. Because the CECAT is composed of items entirely derived from the theory of Karau and Williams, it has construct validity. However, to assess its predictive validity, we asked eighty junior and senior college students to use the summative version of the CECAT to rate two recent experiences they had of being a member of a student team: a satisfactory experience and an unsatisfactory experience. To help the students refresh their memories, before they did their ratings we asked them to write a hundred-word summary of each group experience. To control for unwanted effects of order, half of them rated the satisfactory experience first. Approximately equal numbers of men and women completed the forms. Data from four students were not analyzed because they did not follow instructions. We then conducted statistical tests and correlations to examine the group experiences reported by students.

The results are impressive (see Table 10.1). All but one item (*I expected my coworkers to perform poorly*) significantly discriminated satisfactory from unsatisfactory group experiences. This one bad item was deleted from the CECAT and it does not appear in Tables 10.1 or 10.2. In constructing the CECATs found in Exhibit 10.1, we arranged the items according to their ability to discriminate satisfactory from unsatisfactory experiences. While all the items are associated with significant differences, the first ten items, at this time, appear to be the most important and powerful items. They include the seven items most highly correlated with the level of excellence achieved by the student groups (see Table 10.2).

Suggestions for Using the CECAT. Overall, to set a productive context for using the CECAT, we recommend that instructors heed the practice-based wisdom of those who have used groups, especially the wisdom that is consistent with research and theory on group performance. For example, because tasks make groups, it is a good idea to let the work pick the workers and not to allow students to form their own groups. Hackman (1991) found that groups perform best when they are composed of members who have both a desire and the requisite skills and knowledge to do the group's work. If group members have the desire but not the skill or knowledge, they should learn these things before they join a group (Michaelson and Black, 1994). Also, we strongly urge instructors to grant a high value to group work by giving it sufficient weight in their grading systems and by providing ample in-class time for students to meet. However, grades should not cause conflict within groups. Conflict can be avoided if the goals of each group are clear, evaluation standards for the group and its members are clear, and the instructor evaluates the quality of each group's product while the group members evaluate *one another* on the making of their group's product.

Because the CECAT is prescriptive as well as diagnostic, we recommend that instructors use it (the summative version) in the planning of a course to assess the way they intend to use groups. Changes made before a course begins may be easier to implement than after it is in motion. And to help students learn about working in groups, we urge instructors to administer the CECAT three times: the early version soon after groups are formed, when they are merely discussing and planning their work; the midway version, when the groups have actually begun doing their work; and the summative version, after the groups have made their final presentations or submitted their final products and grades have been assigned.

Table 10.1. Mean Ratings for Satisfactory and Unsatisfactory Group Experiences

CECAT Item	Satisfactory	Unsatisfactory	t
The group performed excellently	4.4	2.2	13.81
Members worked equally hard	3.8	1.7	11.91
The group became more cohesive	4.3	2.2	11.20
I respected my coworkers	4.2	2.2	11.15
Coworkers valued working in a collective	4.0	2.3	10.93
Group outcome was valuable to coworkers	4.1	2.5	10.11
Group outcome was valuable to me	4.1	2.9	7.72
The task was intrinsically interesting	3.8	2.6	7.72
My work was monitored	4.0	2.8	7.62
Performance standards for the group were set	3.8	2.6	6.95
The group was the right size	4.4	3.2	6.36
Performance standards for individuals were set	3.5	2.4	6.03
My effort was instrumental to my outcomes	4.1	3.3	4.89
My performance was evaluated	4.2	3.4	4.65
The task required side-by-side work	3.5	2.6	4.17
I exerted a lot of effort	4.3	3.8	3.60
I contributed resources to the group	4.2	3.8	3.33
My contribution affected the group's outcome	4.0	3.5	3.19
My contribution was unique	3.9	3.4	2.63
The task was challenging	3.7	3.3	2.34

Note: Students rated their experiences on a five-point Likert agree-disagree scale where a 5 was strongly agree. All the above *t*-test results are significant at a minimum of $p < .01$.

Table 10.2. CECAT Items Most Highly Correlated with Group Excellence

CECAT Item	Pearson r
I respected my coworkers	.76
Members worked equally hard	.74
The group became more cohesive	.73
Coworkers valued working in a collective	.71
Group outcome was valuable to coworkers	.65
The group was the right size	.51
My work was monitored	.50
Group outcome was valuable to me	.45
The task was intrinsically interesting	.44
My effort was instrumental to my outcomes	.42
Performance standards for the group were set	.39
My performance was evaluated	.33
The task required side-by-side work	.32
Performance standards for individuals were set	.32
I contributed resources to the group	.31
I exerted a lot of effort	.30
My contribution affected the group's outcome	.27
The task was challenging	.23
My contribution was unique	.19

Note: Correlations equal to or greater than .16 are likely to occur by chance at a probability of .025 with 150 degrees of freedom.

A more detailed recipe for using the CECAT follows.

After the student groups have met a couple of times:

1. Describe and explain the process of using the CECAT, and ask your students whether or not they want to go through this process.
2. If your students want to go through the process, have them complete the "early" version of the CECAT by themselves; they should identify the group they are in, but not reveal their own names.
3. For each group, you, the instructor, should calculate the average total score and the average rating assigned to each item. Letting students see the raw data might compromise their sense of privacy.
4. Then have the groups meet in class and distribute copies of the results to them. Keep these results confidential and within groups.
5. Ask the groups to discuss the results privately and consider the finding that average total scores of 80 and above have been associated with successful, satisfying group experiences and scores of 60 and below have been associated with mediocre performances and unpleasant group experiences, and that mean item ratings of less than 3.0 are diagnostic of specific addressable weaknesses and, conversely, ratings equal to or greater than 4.0 may point to strengths that should be maintained.
6. Finally, visit each group to listen to the students' plans to remedy their weaknesses and build on their strengths. At this point, if it is necessary, you may want to intervene to modify the tasks of the groups or the composition of the groups.

After the groups have worked as intact units for several weeks:

7. Ask your students to complete the "midway" version of the CECAT.
8. Repeat Steps 3, 4, and 5.
9. Ask each group to submit a written summary of its members' discussion of the results and what they plan to do to cope with the problems that the CECAT has identified. Remind them that they are on their own and that you want them to try to solve their problems by themselves *before* they consult with you.

After the groups have completed their work and grades have been assigned:

10. Ask your students to complete the "summative" version of the CECAT.
11. Note what seems to have worked and not worked with the group assignments.

Some Time-Saving Advice and Suggestions. If you are pinched for time, consider using only the "early" and "midway" assessments. Another way to save time is to administer an abbreviated version of the CECAT. The first ten items make up an empirically useful subset; they most clearly distinguish superior from poor group performance. You can also save time by having the teams form reciprocal arrangements with other teams to calculate each other's results, leaving you out of the loop; for example, one member from each team might be asked to tabulate the raw data for a companion team and confidentially share the results with them. If you have students who can not or do not wish to participate in group projects, these students might be asked to serve as "group process assessors." After some training, they would be expected to calculate results for a group or groups and write prescriptive summary reports for them.

Summary

The CECAT is a research- and theory-driven assessment tool. While it embraces what has been found to work with student groups, it has the potential to go beyond this practice-based wisdom and provide insights on *why* certain teaching practices are consistently effective. It can help instructors link basic and applied research, turning their classrooms into labs and thereby enlarging the understanding of all who venture to harness the power of human groups.

References

Abrams, D., and Hogg, M. *Social Identity Theory: Constructive and Theoretical Advances.* New York: Springer-Verlag, 1990.

Bruffee, K. *Collaborative Learning: Higher Education, Interdependence, and the Authority of Knowledge.* Baltimore: Johns Hopkins University Press, 1993.

Cooper, J., and Mueck, R. "Student Involvement in Learning: Cooperative Learning and College Instruction." In A. Goodsell, M. Maher, and V. Tinto (eds.), *Collaborative Learning: A Source Book for Higher Education.* Vol. 1. State College: National Center on Postsecondary Teaching, Learning, and Assessment, Pennsylvania State University, 1992.

Fiechtner, S. B., and Davis, E. A. "Why Some Groups Fail: A Survey of Students' Experiences with Learning Groups." *Organizational Behavior Teaching Review,* 1985, 9 (4), 58–71.

Gamson, Z. F. "Cooperative Learning Comes of Age." In S. Kadel and J. A. Keehner (eds.), *Collaborative Learning: A Source Book for Higher Education.* Vol. 2. State College: National Center on Postsecondary Teaching, Learning, and Assessment, Pennsylvania State University, 1994.

Goethals, G., and Darley, J. "Social Comparison Theory: Self-Evaluations and Group Life." In B. Mullen and G. Goethals (eds.), *Theories of Group Behavior.* New York: Springer-Verlag, 1987.

Hackman, J. R. "Group Influences on Individuals in Organizations." In M. D. Dunnette and L. M. Hough (eds.), *Handbook of Industrial and Organizational Psychology.* (3rd ed.) Palo Alto, Calif.: Consulting Psychologists Press, 1991.

Johnson, D. W., Johnson, R. T., and Holubec, E. *Circles of Learning: Cooperation in the Classroom.* Edina, Minn.: Interaction Book Company, 1990.

Kadel, S., and Keehner, J. A. *Collaborative Learning: A Source Book for Higher Education.* Vol. 2. State College: National Center on Postsecondary Teaching, Learning, and Assessment, Pennsylvania State University, 1994.

Karau, S. J., and Williams, K. D. "Social Loafing: A Meta-Analytical Review and Theoretical Integration." *Journal of Personality and Social Psychology,* 1993, 65, 681–706.

Karau, S. J., and Williams, K. D. "Social Loafing: Research Findings, Implications, and Future Directions." *Current Directions in Psychological Science,* 1995, 4 (5), 134–140.

Kravitz, D. A., and Martin, B. "Ringlemann Rediscovered: The Original Article." *Journal of Personality and Social Psychology,* 1986, 50, 936–941.

Michaelson, L. K., and Black, R. H. "Building Learning Teams: The Key to Harnessing the Power of Small Groups in Education." In S. Kadel and J. A. Keehner (eds.), *Collaborative Learning: A Source Book for Higher Education.* Vol. 2. State College: National Center on Postsecondary Teaching, Learning, and Assessment, Pennsylvania State University, 1994.

Slavin, R. E. *Cooperative Learning: Theory, Research, and Practice.* Upper Saddle River, N.J.: Prentice Hall, 1990.

Smith, K. A., Johnson, D. W., and Johnson, R. T. "Cooperative Learning and Positive Change in Higher Education." In A. Goodsell, M. Maher, and V. Tinto (eds.), *Collaborative Learning: A Source Book for Higher Education.* Vol. 1. State College: National Center on Postsecondary Teaching, Learning, and Assessment, Pennsylvania State University, 1992.

Walker, C. J. "Assessing Group Process: Using Classroom Assessment to Build Autonomous Learning Teams." *Assessment Update,* 1995, 7 (6), 4–5.

CHARLES WALKER is professor of psychology at St. Bonaventure University.

THOMAS ANGELO is associate professor and director of the Assessment Center at the School for New Learning, DePaul University.

INDEX

Abrams, D., 103
Accountability, 5–6, 87–88
Accounting, CATs used in classes in, 37–45
Accounting Education Change Commission (AECC), 37–38
Administration, support from, 52–54, 97
American Accounting Association (AAA), 37
Angelo, T. A., 1, 6, 8, 14, 15, 17, 23, 26, 29, 32, 33, 40, 41, 44, 47, 53, 60, 61, 67, 82, 91, 92, 95
Arthur Andersen & Co., 37
Arthur Young, 37
Assessment: for accountability vs. improvement, 5–6; formative vs. summative, 68, 87–88; of group work, 103–111; student involvement in, 6; Winthrop University program for, 88–89
Association of American Colleges, 60
Atkinson, P. E., 52
Attention, cognitive learning theory on, 14

Background knowledge probes, 42, 83
Beard, V., 38
Berry, E., 51, 53
Black, R. H., 102, 108
Bloom, B. S., 11, 39
Bogue, E. G., 47
Boyer, E. L., 59
Brooks, K. O., 91
Brown, O. H., 79
Bruffee, K., 102

California State University at San Marcos (CSUSM), CATs related to disciplines at, 60–65
Carnegie Foundation for the Advancement of Teaching, 29
Categorizing grids: and cognitive theory, 15; used by teaching assistants, 83, 84, 85
Catlin, A., 23, 27
Cerbin, W., 82
Chickering, A. W., 60
Classroom Assessment: advantages/disadvantages for faculty/students, 26–31; as formative assessment, 68; pegagogy supporting, 60; systemwide implementation of, 67–77; as total quality management (TQM), 47–54; vs. Classroom Research, 8. *See also* Classroom Assessment Techniques (CATs); Classroom Research
Classroom Assessment Handbook (Angelo and Cross), 17
Classroom Assessment Techniques: A Handbook for College Teachers (Angelo and Cross), 23, 33, 53, 67–68
Classroom Assessment Techniques (CATs): in accounting classes, 37–45; and cognitive learning theory, 13–15, 33; to develop teaching assistants' skills, 79–86; to enhance learning, 15–19; feedback provided by, 7–8; purposes for using, 34, 48; related to disciplines, 60–65; studies of, in community colleges, 23–33; to teach learning strategies, 17, 18, 19, 31–33; teacher/student involvement in, 6. *See also specific techniques*
Classroom Research: Early Lessons from Success (Angelo), 1
Classroom Research: Implementing the Scholarship of Teaching (Cross and Steadman), 14, 33
Classroom Research, 5–12; as community-building, 11–12; example of project cycle for, 9–10; improving teaching using, 53–54; related to disciplines, 8–9; simple sources for, 10–11; systemwide implementation of, 67–77; vs. Classroom Assessment, 8; vs. research, 9, 68–69; Winthrop University program for, 88, 90–98. *See also* Classroom Assessment
Cognitive learning theory, 13–19, 33; applied to specific CATs, 15–19; connection-building processes identified by, 14, 15; learning more about, 17–18
Cohen, D. K., 59
Cohen, J., 38
Collective Effort Classroom Assessment Technique (CECAT), 103–111; recommendations on using, 108, 110–111; sample instruments for, 104–106

Back Issue/Subscription Order Form

Copy or detach and send to:
Jossey-Bass Inc., Publishers, 350 Sansome Street, San Francisco CA 94104-1342

Call or fax toll free!
Phone 888-378-2537 6AM-5PM PST; Fax 800-605-2665

Back issues: Please send me the following issues at $23 each
(Important: please include series initials and issue number, such as TL90)

1. TL _____

_____

_____

$ _____ Total for single issues

$ _____ Shipping charges (for single issues *only;* subscriptions are exempt from shipping charges): Up to $30, add $5^{50} • $30^{01}–$50, add $6^{50} $50^{01}–$75, add $7^{50} • $75^{01}–$100, add $9 • $100^{01}–$150, add $10 Over $150, call for shipping charge

Subscriptions   Please ❏ start   ❏ renew my subscription to *New Directions for Teaching and Learning* for the year 19___ at the following rate:

❏ Individual $56   ❏ Institutional $99
NOTE: Subscriptions are quarterly, and are for the calendar year only. Subscriptions begin with the spring issue of the year indicated above. For shipping outside the U.S., please add $25.

$ _____ Total single issues and subscriptions (CA, IN, NJ, NY and DC residents, add sales tax for single issues. NY and DC residents must include shipping charges when calculating sales tax. NY and Canadian residents only, add sales tax for subscriptions)

❏ Payment enclosed (U.S. check or money order only)

❏ VISA, MC, AmEx, Discover Card #_____ Exp. date_____

Signature _____ Day phone _____

❏ Bill me (U.S. institutional orders only. Purchase order required)

Purchase order #_____

Name _____

Address _____

_____

_____

Phone_____ E-mail _____

For more information about Jossey-Bass Publishers, visit our Web site at:
www.josseybass.com   **PRIORITY CODE – ND1**

OTHER TITLES AVAILABLE IN THE NEW DIRECTIONS FOR TEACHING AND LEARNING SERIES
Robert J. Menges, Editor-in-Chief
Marilla D. Svinicki, Associate Editor

Printed in the United States
64640LVS00004B/101